MISS LILLIAN TALKING:

"WHEN PEOPLE WANT TO KNOW WHAT MAKES JIMMY TICK, WHAT INFLUENCE I HAD ON MY CHILDREN, I TELL THEM IT WAS JUST A DAY-BY-DAY INFLUENCE. BUT I DID TELL MY CHILDREN ONE THING: ALWAYS DO WHAT YOU THINK IS RIGHT, AND DON'T PAY ANY ATTENTION TO CRITICISM."

"I'M A CHRISTIAN, THE WAY I SEE IT. BUT I DO A LOT OF THINGS THE LADIES OF THE CHURCH THINK I SHOULDN'T DO. I SMOKE WHEN I WANT TO. I TAKE A DRINK LATE IN THE EVENING . . . THERE ARE JUST SO MANY THINGS THAT I DO THAT LONG-FACED, DYED-IN-THE-WOOL CHRISTIANS DO NOT DO."

"AS TO BEING A WIDOW, GO AND GET YOUR JOB THE MINUTE YOUR HUSBAND DIES AND STAY BUSY! THAT IS THE ONLY HOPE. . . . I SPEAK TO RETIRED PEOPLE, AND I MAKE FUN OF THEM FOR RETIRING AT 62 IF THEY'RE IN GOOD HEALTH. I HAD TO HELP WITH THE BUSINESS BECAUSE I KNEW MORE ABOUT IT THAN JIMMY DID."

No one can ever think of Lillian Carter merely as "Jimmy Carter's mother"—though a lot of folks in Plains will tell you that Jimmy Carter is "Miss Lillian's boy." Now is your chance to meet this most remarkable lady face to face—and enjoy a wit and wisdom you will never forget.

Big Bestsellers from SIGNET

Miss Lillian and Friends:

The Plains, Georgia, Family Philosophy and Recipe Book

AS TOLD TO
Beth Tartan
AND
Rudy Hayes

A SIGNET BOOK
NEW AMERICAN LIBRARY
TIMES MIRROR

Library of Congress Catalog Card Number: 76-55941

This is an authorized reprint of a hardcover edition published by A & W
Publishers, Inc.

Front cover photo by Charles M. Rafshoon (Pictorial Parade).

First Signet Printing, September, 1977

1 2 3 4 5 6 7 8 9

Contents

Foreword

Having a core of my existence that never changed, results in a given counsel with friends and neighbors. The special events of life form a common vantage point that has been a stable factor in my life.

The fact that both my and Rosalynn's ancestors who have lived in Plains were born in the 1700's, gives me a frame of reference in which to answer the impact of changing times.

Here you get to know people who are representative of the American public.

With land and religion and the forces of the society here, of life here, you have unchanging principles that are very reassuring. You have very high standards of morality that are demanded. One is expected to be kind to each other, to work hard, and to pay one's debts.

If you don't, it is obvious to people whose opinion you value.

Jimmy Carter
PRESIDENT
UNITED STATES OF AMERICA

III. Plato's Way of Life

Acknowledgments

Without the people of Plains this book would not have been possible. They have patiently borne with the nation as it has examined, pried, probed, and analyzed their folkways. It is hoped that they will recognize themselves in this book, and greet it with the same air of common sense and Southern hospitality with which they have treated so many visitors during an historical year.

This combination of grace and practicality comes naturally to the people of Plains and to one of its leading citizens, Miss Lillian Carter, who has given unstintingly of her time and energy in countless interviews in her home so that the reader—the visitor to Plains—could gain a better understanding of the town, of its customs, and, of course, of her son, President Jimmy Carter.

The entire Carter clan is to be thanked; their in-laws; and all their friends. In short, a bow to the 638 citizens of Plains, Ga.

For the inspiration for this book and unstinting work in pursuing it to a successful conclusion, credit is due Michael J. Hamilton, executive editor of Cahners Books, Int., Boston, Mass. There are also many who helped along the way: Bruce Petri for his wit and consulting skills; Marcia Lebow for her intelligence, research ability, and culinary skills; and Zelda Fischer of the Word Guild, Cambridge, Mass., who helped to see that the project was successfully guided through its various editorial stages.

But most of all, this is the story of the people of Plains, of the life they live and of their good humor, practicality, and grace under a variety of demanding circumstances. It is they who have had the faith to work hard for a cause in which they believe; and it is they who have succeeded.

I. Miss Lillian

The nation's grandmother. Creamy white hair with a touch of steel. Dancing blue eyes in an impish face. Well-won lines and high cheekbones. A brown birthmark above her right jaw. Sturdy. Energetic. A demeanor not to be argued with; a free-thinker who can speak her mind with a charm that beggars disagreement. The President's mother:

> I told him to quit that stuff about never telling lies and being a Christian and how he loves his wife more than the day he met her. There are some things you don't have to go around saying.[1]

Two-piece pants suits in white or bright colors: sky blue; canary yellow; maroon; and, of course, light, bright Carter green:

> I'm an integrationist. Jimmy's father wasn't. I try to be tolerant of everyone even people from Alabama.[2]

Cuss words now and then, when the bugs are eating the grass. Fishing for relaxation, and watching the squirrels scramble up and down the Georgia pine:

> Do I ever lie? Oh, yes. I couldn't live without it.[3]

Small feet in dark blue canvas shoes, pushing the rocker back and forth, back and forth, as she talks:

> All I'm going to say about abortion—because it's pro and con on that—is that I think a woman's body should be hers. I don't believe in getting pregnant and aborting and things like that, but I think that should be whatever she desires. I believe in women having equal rights, and I think that's one of them.[4]

The house is set back about 100 feet from U.S. 280, with a flat front yard and healthy but not manicured lawn. A one-story, modest brick house with a porte-cochere on the left shading a blue four-door Caprice classic, with oaks on the sides and a grey poodle playing by the slight row of shrubbery in the front:

> I've always been for the underdog. I've always been able to do, financially, anything I wanted to do, and I had just as soon help a black person as a white. And in Plains, I've been asked to do things that no other woman would be asked to do for the blacks, like speaking to the school or speaking at the church. And I'm sure that—they don't say it out loud—but I get criticized for those things.[5]

The rocker is set in a small opening by the door of the house; a long line is waiting. A sign behind the rocker says "Please Do Not Shake Hand":

> On the whole, although I have not liked some of the things he has said or done, I have so much faith in Jimmy as a man, not just as my son. I know I am prejudiced, but looking at all the candidates this time—and I never miss a trick—I have seen that he is head and shoulders above them.[6]

The line edges along. An old man touches his hat and smiles a greeting. A little girl hands her a pad. "Jimmy's Mama," she signs. The line gets shorter until there is no one left. "Don't trip on the front step, now," she says as the last visitor takes leave. She opens the screen door, settles into the soft yellow-and-brown striped couch and motions toward the yellow chair, the lady who has captured the imagination of America; the lady who at 68 entered the Peace Corps and journeyed to India to put her nursing training to good use; the lady who speaks her mind and enjoys a chance to do it; the lady who—

"You hush!"

What?

"Sit down, you are on my time now."

Ladies and gentlemen, Miss Lillian Carter!

"When people want to know what makes Jimmy tick, what influence I had on my children, I tell them it was just a day-by-day influence. But I did tell my children one thing: Always do what you think is right, and don't pay any attention to criticism. . . .

"I'm a Christian, the way I see it. But I do a lot of things the ladies of the church think I shouldn't do. I smoke when I want to. I take a drink late in the evening; I used to do it with my husband before he died, and I still do. I'm allergic to tranquilizers; I'm allergic to everything except my little drink of bourbon. But there are just so many things that I do that long-faced, dyed-in-the-wool Christians do not do. . . .

"I tell you, here's a good way to sum it up. I go to church on Sunday, but I don't think all churchgoers are Christians. I think there's a difference between religion and Christianity.

"My kindness to the underdogs in Georgia has always been criticized by people. But, thank goodness, I can go to bed at night and go to sleep thinking: 'I haven't done anybody any wrong.' How can people who say they are Christians be so cruel?"[7]

Or:

"I suppose I feel like any mother would whose son is so close to such high achievement. But you know, it's come so easily we've been able to accustom ourselves gradually to the idea that he'll be president. Perhaps if he'd had a hard time and stumbled a bit at first there might be a stranger feeling about it now. But people in other parts of the country apparently feel as we do—that Jimmy'll make a wonderful president, the best we've ever had."[8]

Later, on September 22, 1976, the day of the first debate between then-President Gerald Ford and Jimmy Carter:

I'll tell you, I had another house and twelve years ago it burned and a lot of pictures and a lot of books burned with it. I've been trying to find pictures of Christmas for religious magazines, and all of them were destroyed by fire.

We're very traditional: we had a Christmas tree. My husband and the children would go out and cut a tree and we'd decorate it a week before Christmas. Out there the house wasn't too warm. We heated everything before fireplaces; we had to warm ourselves by heaters, so that the house didn't get too hot and the tree would last a week without getting too brittle. We'd decorate it a week before Christmas. Then we would have all the gifts under the tree, except the children would hang their stockings. We had a mantle—a place set for the stockings.

Christmas dinner was prepared the day before. Fortunately my cook wanted to be there, so we had turkey and dressing. We had a good time. We never had turkey except on Thanksgiving and Christmas. And then when we had company, turkey was the biggest thing we could get.

As to my influence on my children, I am very modest about that. I'll tell you, my husband had a great influence over Jimmy and Ruth [the youngest girl, five years younger than Jimmy]. He's been dead 22 years. It's difficult to go back and remember every little thing, but I'm sure he did. He thought Ruth was the most beautiful thing on earth and he told her that every day, and she was. I try to be modest. I'm sure that I influenced them in their reading. Not direct influence, but as they looked at me they would know that I read. I never censored their reading.

I fish, I play cards, I look at television, and I read. I could live with just reading. My father read, my mother read. But it's not tradition, it's just a habit. I read anything on earth. Now I like political books. I've always liked politics, and I guess my choice would be political books. I've gone through a stage with Russian novels when I didn't want to read anything else.

His teacher, Miss Julia Coleman, recommended *War and Peace* to him. She was a crippled lady and she oversaw his reading at school. She had a great influence on his reading at school, but at the house every book that came out I bought. I belong to two or three book clubs and children's book clubs. Well, his godmother we call her, when Jimmy was born, October 1st and on Christmas, she gave him the complete set of the Book of Knowledge and also of Guy de Maupassant. His godmother gave him those. He saved them. She gave him those books to start his library and he has them in his library there.

I don't have glasses, but I have contacts. I've had two operations on both eyes. I wear contacts, but if I read in small print, I can read a paper without them. I have 20-20 vision using contacts following my operation. That's pretty good.

A happy family, that's what we had—a very happy family. When the children were small, we had nights when we had a family prayer. My husband would read a chapter from the Bible, and we'd have a prayer. It was just a normal thing, not a big deal. We'd do this every night until the children got old enough to date. Before bedtime.

My children learned they all had their chores to do. Jimmy had his chores. They got paid for them, by the way. I don't think he mentioned that in the book [*Why Not the Best?*].

I have four children, and they are all very fine children (two of them are not as religious as the other two, but that doesn't take away their value). They had a good home life, and lived with a mother and father daily who are more or less Christian people; and in those days they had no temptation. Can you understand that? They had no temptation. They had to go to school at 7:30 in the morning, come home at 3:30 in the afternoon. They didn't have a beer joint, they didn't have anything to tempt them. When they went to the movies, we took them on Saturday or Sunday afternoon. I remember all of us sitting around—Jimmy always laid down on a stump to read—but all of us reading. We'd just have orgies reading.

When they played, they played outside in the big yard and they had playmates mostly among the black children. We lived out in the section where there were no white children, and they played ball. Gloria and Ruth had a little black girl they played dolls with. Jimmy had his buddy [the black, A.D. Davis], and they built a tree house, and they would go fishing in the woods. There was nothing to teach them bad habits, you might say; and so a child that grows up in that environment never picks up bad habits. They never knew about drugs. I didn't either. Can you understand that?

My husband and I went to a lot of parties, and we would take a drink if we wanted to; but the children didn't. They didn't know anything about that.

As the years went by, my husband bought one farm and he'd buy one piece of property and sell it, and he would help people who wanted to buy a farm. He would furnish the money to buy a farm and then after he got sick, he'd canceled so many of those notes. But when he died, he left considerable property for us. That was from the time Jimmy was seven until Earl died in 1953, after Jimmy had married and had two children.

Earl was very successful. He started off with $100 a month. We managed and saved money with it, and we bought a farm. He bought the first one on credit and then he was a successful farmer and he paid for that. Then he bought another farm, and after he had bought the second or third farm, we never had anything on credit. Everything—we paid cash for everything. He was very successful. He was in the peanut business years before he died, and the fertilizer business, too.

I had one man come and all we talked about was my husband. We've had tourists who wanted autographs come through here from all over the world, but Sunday before last I did 1800 autographs. You can see the crowds that we've had. When they find out that Jimmy's not going to be here this Sunday, not as many are going to come. A lot of them want to come here, spend the night, and go to church on Sunday to hear him teach the Bible class.

So much has been made of religion. It wasn't too much with us. We were Baptists, and we went to church. The church is the center of everything in a small town, even the entertainment, and it was just more of a habit to go to church. And then Jimmy joined the church. It wasn't a bid deal. All my children joined the church when they were around 11 or 12 years old.

As to being a widow, Go to get your job the minute your husband dies and stay busy! That is the only hope. I made so many talks about this. Since I went to India, I've made over 600. I speak to retired people, and I make fun of them for retiring at 62 if they're in good health. I had to help with the business because I knew more about it than Jimmy did. Then I went to Auburn, and I was a housemother for 7½ years, and that got me over the hump.

When I told my children I was doing it, they thought it was horrible. I had never left Plains _for_ anything. I had never made a nickel outside of the business except the three or four years that I had training. I nursed some. Jimmy said, "Mother, if you go in—and you've got to go—I want you to have the prettiest car in Auburn." And this sounds ridiculous, but he said, "I want you to take the money"—they have to pay you something—it was $125—"I want you to spend it all on the boys. I want you to be the Mother of all those boys and let them come to you as a Mother." He was telling me in a subtle sort of way to get over my husband's death. It didn't take me six months before I was completely acclimated. I have never ceased being lonely for him, but I've never been lonely for anyone else.

I had a Cadillac and I let the boys use it. They came to me with problems. They would come into my sitting room to leave notes: "Lillian, may I see you at twelve o'clock? I have a problem." Or, "May I see you at noon?" I had dates with the boys up until midnight. I forgot my problems, don't you see?

Ever since then, when I think I'm going to get in a rut or get old, something happens to boost me. I'm old but I'm young at heart, and I'm active. I had my eyes operated on. I've had cataracts. I had one operated on and three years later the other. And now this, Jimmy running for President. I wouldn't advise you to have a son running for President. I'll tell you it isn't easy.

Jimmy asked me to come down and meet these people who come. They want to meet somebody in this family. It is surprising when I get out of the car downtown. I can't walk down the street without people surrounding me. "Wait a minute, there she is!" They know me from television. "I'm coming down at one o'clock. Can you wait until one o'clock?"

I've just opened 62 letters this morning with my secretary, and the most difficult thing is learning not to worry about every letter. I've learned that if a letter doesn't have a return address on the back, I throw it in the wastebasket because it doesn't have to be answered; and I open something else. It's very difficult to be able to stay calm during the day, and then prepare for the activity and all these other things. But I love meeting people.

I've been there where I've had a hundred people waiting, and on Sunday I have a helper (he's a man about 45 years old who comes in from the country to organize them) to get them in line. He tells them to get in line, don't shake her hand, and just don't rush. And I sit and I sign autographs, and I try to see everybody. If there are a hundred people there, I can't sign all. I say, "Where are you from?" And I sign and autograph.

It's inspiring to me to look out from my car across the street and someone yells, "Wait a minute!" I say, "I'm going right over there and I'll be in my chair in a few minutes." These people tell their relatives, and I've had so many phone calls asking, "Are you going to be there Sunday? If you're not, we don't want to make the trip." Now, that is not being very humble, but it's not being—I'm not egotistical. They just want to see me; they just want to see somebody in Jimmy's family. They know they can't see him, and I'm the next best thing.

While I'm not as deeply religious as Jimmy is, the very thought of anything else other than God never enters my mind. I'm a great believer in prayer and the one prayer I have is to take care of my children. To take care of Jimmy, and make him be able to say the right thing at the right time. Sometimes he doesn't, but to let him get through with this race is very important to Jimmy and I. I keep the little girl. She's eight years old and my whole life now is for her, seeing that nothing happens to her, getting her clothes ready. I just know that God has taken care of Jimmy through this so far. And me. And when my time comes, I think I'll be ready to go.

I have never had dreams of Jimmy being President of the United States, but since he's gotten into this, just let me be able to help as much as I can. I used to get up at five o'clock in the morning and go everywhere and get back at twelve at night. But now I have promised Jimmy that I would keep Amy. She doesn't have a Mother and Father every day, but she has her grandma; and she is old enough to understand the seriousness of it. I teach her every day why they can't be with her all the time, and she knows. She has another grandmother in town, but she's different from me. She's shy and she's very sweet and a very good woman; but Jimmy says, "Mother, if you'll keep Amy with you, you'll never have a worry." He knows that I'm a strong person and that I would give my life for Amy. Now she has to have a bodyguard in school, but I get up at five o'clock and I dismiss the bodyguard, because we're surrounded with Secret Service.

Last Saturday afternoon, I had a man from *Newsweek* come down. He took 500 different photographs of me in about an hour and a half for the future. I said, "Do you line the walls with them?" "No," he said, "we keep them for a psychological moment." So I'm accustomed to that, and nearly everyone who comes for an autograph, comes for a picture. Sometimes I sit still, sometimes I sit on the porch. I'm very accomodating.

I'm not dreading the debate too much. I had people come from all over the United States—papers, magazines, UPI, AP, all of them: "Would it be possible if I sent someone to your house to watch you in the debate?" And I said no. I had one man who was very insistent, but I don't want anybody. They only want to come out of curiosity to see how I respond.

I don't want a friend. Amy'll be there. My sons, they'll be looking through their own televisions. No friend would be as interested as I. They'd take every mood: if I looked sad or if I had to go to the bathroom. I don't trust them, you see.

Do you know what Jimmy said to me? "Mother, don't worry about the debates. I have it all under control," and I said, "I'm glad." And I said, "Goodbye and good luck." I had the opportunity to talk to him for three hours, and I didn't say a word to him. I went up—I stayed here at Jimmy's last night—I went up at six thirty to get Amy ready for school because I knew I had to stay here the rest of the time and I just had two nights at home. I just love to sleep in my own bed. So I took the papers in to him, and I said, "Did you sleep well?" And he said, "Yes. Sit down." And I said, "No. I don't want to. I've got to get Amy up." So he was sitting in the living room reading, going over some of his material and I said, "Bye, good luck." . . . He's my child. I know his brain is working. I know that anything I say takes his thoughts off of what he's doing.

II. Miss Lillian, Matriarch

Lillian Gordy Carter, Southern matriarch, head of the clan, Mother of the President, was born in 1898 in Richland, Georgia, a small town about twenty miles from

Plains. Her father, Jim Jack Gordy, was "the best, biggest
politician in this part of the world. He kept up with politics so closely that he could tell you—almost within five
votes—what the people who were running would get in
the next election. And so he was very popular."[1]

Gordy was a friend of Tom Watson, an excitable popu-
list who attempted in the 1890's to lead the poor
white and the downtrodden black of the South in a
crusade against the overbearing Whigs of the region.
When he failed, he railed at the blacks for being ungrate-
ful and lambasted the Yankees for their "monastic gloom,
nasal preachments, kill-joy countenances, lank-haired bigotry and censorious intermeddling with everybody's
business."[2]

"Grandpa never ran for public office himself," writes
Carter, "but was the postmaster during four different
presidential administrations, and later was federal district
revenue officer. This required nimble political footwork
because at that time there was no civil service system. To
the winners went the spoils." And Gordy was progressive.
He came up with the idea of Rural Free Mail Delivery
and made it a reality by prodding his friend (and congressman) Watson to get the necessary federal legislation
passed.[3]

When she came over to Plains from Richland to learn
to be a nurse under the tutelage of Dr. Sam Wise, Lillian
had been dating a boy named George Tanner. Dr. Sam
took her aside: "I don't like you going out with him. I'll
tell you who I would like you to go with. It's Earl Carter.
He's a boy that has more ambition than anybody in this
town, and he's going to be worth a lot some day."[4]

They went to Americus to see a production of Shake-
speare's *The Merchant of Venice* on their first date; but
she almost couldn't bring herself to go in. "It cost five
dollars a seat, and we felt just terrible." She said she
didn't want to go, but Earl retorted: "Well, we're going.

We're already here." "So we saw the play," she says. "It was a beautiful play and I enjoyed it—especially Portia."[5] (They followed the dating customs of the times, and it was two months before she allowed Earl to kiss her, although now she says: "I'm broad-minded about a lot of things. I don't criticize people living together before they're married. I kind of take it in stride. It's just the way of the world now. . . .")[6]

Earl Carter himself had a family tree that had distinguished ancestors hanging on it like Spanish moss. Some relatives trace the Carter line back to the unofficially knighted Sir Thomas Carter, who set foot in America in 1650 (indeed, some relatives claim, through Carter's wife, Catherine Dale, kinship to Alfred the Great of England). A few generations later, James Carter of Virginia (born 1737) was fighting in the Revolutionary War. The line of direct descendants gradually drifts west, first to Warrenton, in east Georgia; and next to Schley County, eleven miles from Plains, where Wiley Carter took up homesteading. He married Ann Ansley, had twelve children, and left them all sizeable tracts of land.[7]

> "Land is the only thing in the world that amounts to anything," he shouted, his thick, short arms making wide gestures of indignation, "for 'tis the only thing in this world that lasts; and don't you be forgetting it! 'Tis the only thing worth working for, worth fighting for—worth dying for."
>
> "Oh, Pa," she said disgustedly, "you talk like an Irishman!"
>
> "Have I ever been ashamed of it? No, 'tis proud I am. And don't be forgetting that you are half Irish, Miss! And to anyone with a drop of Irish blood in them the land they live on is like their mother. . . ."
>
> —Mr. Gerald to Scarlett O'Hara,
> *Gone With the Wind* by Margaret Mitchell[8]

The Carters with their Scotch-Irish blood also seem to have a love of the land, and an ability to acquire it.[9] Not only did Mr. Earl continually purchase new lands and farms, and help others to do so, but in his early years, his son Jimmy was also showing the same propensity, as he wrote in *Why Not the Best?*:

> I got to be a businessman in those days, on a small scale, even if it seemed on a big scale for me. I would earn about $1 per day gross income selling peanuts, and on Saturdays sometimes I could sell as much as five times that amount. By the time I was nine years old I had saved enough money to purchase five bales of cotton at the then all-time low price of five cents per pound. I kept this cotton in one of my daddy's farm storehouses until the price increased after a few years to eighteen cents, at which time I sold it for enough money to purchase five houses, owned at the time by the estate of the recently deceased local undertaker. From then until I left home to enter the Naval Academy, I collected $16.50 in rent each month from those five houses. Two rented for $5 each, two for $2 each, and one for $2.50. The houses were finally sold to the tenants in 1949 while I was living in Hawaii as a naval officer.[10]

The family of Mr. Earl and Miss Lillian grew, with her at the focal point. Always there was Mother, "the matriarch of our family," as Jimmy writes, who "provided a nucleus around which our different individual families revolved. She is an extrovert, very dynamic, inquisitive in her attitude about life, compassionate toward others, and has had a wide variety of experiences even in her advancing years."[11]

There were four children in the family, "all different

personalities," says Miss Lillian, "and I'm proud of each of them for different reasons."[12] The oldest is Jimmy, now 52 and nicknamed "Hot" (quick moving—the Secret Service calls him "Dasher"; ambitious, a "hot shot"; or, as Mr. Earl would say [quoted by Jimmy]: "Hot, would you like to turn the potato vines this morning?"); two years younger is Gloria Carter Spann, nicknamed "Gogo" (free spirit, motorcycle enthusiast); five years younger is Ruth Carter Stapleton, nicknamed "Boopy Doop" (Mr. Earl thought she was the prettiest); and, finally, there is the feisty Billy, thirteen years younger and succinctly nicknamed "Buck."[13]

Miss Lillian recalls when Jimmy told her of his political ambitions: "I had been staying in the Governor's Mansion in Atlanta about four years ago, recovering from a broken shoulder. Jimmy came into my room one night and said, 'Mama, I'm going to run for president.'

"I was so startled I said, 'president of what?'

"He said, 'President of the United States.'

"I told him, 'Jimmy, that's a big undertaking.' He knew it was, but told me he was going to work hard and he was going to win. Not that I ever doubted his ability. But the chances seemed so remote. There hasn't been a president elected from the deep South since before the Civil War. There's so much prejudice, and there were so many other people more well-known nationally. . . ."[14]

Sister Gloria hints at what helped Jimmy succeed in his quest: "He's a very disciplined person. We have one thing in common—I don't know if anybody else in the family does it or not—but I've always made a schedule and he always has a schedule. From the time he started working down at the warehouse he'd have a schedule written out of the things to do that day. Now he does this, now he does that; he goes right down his schedule and sees that everything gets done. I don't know whether the Navy did that or his determination to get into Annapolis—he needed to gain weight and did his studying in bed so his energy would all go to weight—to be absolutely certain he had the marks, the grades, the classes, everything. This was an imposed discipline."[15]

"They call her the 'motorcycle fiend,' " says Miss Lillian of Gloria.[16] Now she'll get a chance to defend her passion as a lobbyist in Washington on behalf of the motorcycle industry, a rumored wish.

"And then Ruth—I just love Ruth," says Lillian. "We're so proud of her evangelism. Some papers call her a 'faith healer,' but it isn't that at all. She was originally a Baptist ... But she thinks that the church is a narrow place and so she's not really affiliated with any church now. She is her own church, you might say."[17]

Miss Lillian seeks to explain her younger daughter: "Ruth wasn't very religious when she was young. Jimmy wasn't. It's normal to be a member of the church when you're small. Jimmy has always been a Christian and he says his Christianity is like breathing, and it is with Ruth, too. Ruth just went to church on Sunday casually. She married when she was in the senior class at school. After she married—and I'm telling you how she got religion— they moved to North Carolina. He's a veterinarian, and he went into business with Ruth's first cousin, and she had four children, close together. She has a small frame and is not a very strong person. I mean, she doesn't look strong. She had four children right straight along and she became very depressed after the last child was born; not seriously, but too much for her. The pediatrician who was tending the child advised her to go into psychiatry, which she did.

"She went into psychoanalysis, one of those groups. She loved it. She went about four months, and I understand in a group of eight, you cannot come out, even if you are cured, even if the psychiatrist pronounces you well, until all eight are better. So Ruth went on, and I think in eight months or something like that she was out of there.

"Then she went to this religious meeting of C.F.O. in Hendersonville, North Carolina. They always had it at a beautiful spot. It was out in the mountains, and it was founded by a Methodist preacher who thought that religion was too narrow, which it is. He thought to have a church, a place that everybody could go to, that was nondenominational. He was a Methodist preacher, but this was nondenominational. You'd go to a beautiful spot. They always had these meetings in a very beautiful spot. A man can play golf, you can go swimming—all these things at every camp, so you don't have to go to a meeting if you don't want to. Nobody cares. You dress casually. This has been going on for twenty years or more. So she got interested in that religion, which is this: The only way I can explain her religion to you is to say "the love of God, the love of Christ, the love of Jesus and your love for him and not hell and damnation"—that's what she preaches. She preaches that if you are a Christian like she is a Christian, the love of Christ will do anything for you. And they do not preach hell and damnation, so I love that, too. I went to a lot of those meetings, and they are all over the world. She became a speaker in that faith, and she's gone much deeper now. That's her right. She did not get that from me."

And then there's the gregarious Billy, who, in his mother's way of cussing, vowed to "tear down that damn tree" (the plastic one put up in Plains for Christmas), as a campaign promise in the mayoral election in the small town (he lost but lived to hear about the night he was out of town and someone hooked a car up to the tree and hauled it off).[18] Billy manages the peanut business. Billy is in town. Billy is good for a laugh, but he is also shrewd; and he and Miss Lillian understand one another: "Billy is the most important child to me in the family," she says, "because he looks after the whole operation and he looks after me. He does all my finances. I don't have to pay a big bill. He's busy right now because it's the peanut season, and then he has a 'No Admittance' sign up. People like to drive him crazy, just walking in."

Billy is indeed a good interview, and when asked about his brother he says: ". . . I would say that he's extremely honest and believes in what he's doing. I have heard reports that he's hardheaded, and he is hardheaded until you convince him that your way is better than his. He is flexible but you just have to know more about the subject and convince him. He's not as one-way as the press has led everybody to believe on that. My temper is a lot worse than his but when we disagree over some policy or some piece of machinery, both of us get over it real fast. I'm more of a red-neck than Jimmy, and some of our biggest arguments have been over the way I handled some of the black labor. But I have changed lately."[19]

There promise to be other changes in the South, changes long coming, changes accelerated by the dignity brought to the region by having one of its own President. As Sen. Ernest F. Hollings of South Carolina said, "We've got Carter. Now we can rejoin the Union."[20]

In the new racial attitudes, the new hope for the future, there lies Miss Lillian's past. Like any good matriarch, she set the pace for her family. As befits a woman who has raised a President, she has also set the pace of the nation: "When Johnson ran for President after Kennedy died, I was a delegate to the national convention and loved it, had a ball. And I came home, and they asked me if I would be cochairman of the campaign office for Johnson. At that time [1964], people around here didn't like Johnson because he was for the blacks, and they called him a N-I-G-G-E-R lover, you know. Anyway, I was delighted to do it, took the job, and the blacks had access to the office over at the hotel just like whites. That was days before we thought too much about integration. And when I'd come down and get in my car in the afternoon, there would be spots all over it where somebody had thrown something against it. Occasionally they would throw something at the car when I was in it, but never to hit me, just to hit the car. Even the boys and girls of my friends would just yell things. They wouldn't let me know who was yelling it, but they yelled. It didn't bother me. Johnson won. And I won out on that one."[21]

There was nursing blacks and whites alike; there was trying for equality and speaking one's mind. It rankled the neighbors, and even today, beneath the buoyancy of Plains and the Carter boom, jealous, angry voices can be heard. A sample of many, from a white woman shopping in Turner's hardware store: "Lillian Carter always thought she was better than us. She always felt she was a great reader. She brought up that church-integration thing in 1954 [it was 1965], just so she could show us up. She didn't want colored people in there any more than we did. She thinks she is so smart and we're so dumb. . . ."[22]

This is the reverse side of the small-town pastoral image, and it's the small-town world of pressure and, at times, bigotry: If you rock the boat, watch out! Miss Lillian, being a nurse who treated blacks, was continually under fire; and Jimmy received his share, too. Besides the church argument, Jimmy became embroiled in a controversy over the White Citizens' Council. When he refused to join, the social pressure was turned on. A picture emerges in Jimmy's own words in *Why Not the Best?*: "I repeated my statement that I did not wish to join, and eventually they left again.

"After a few more days, they came back with several of my close friends, some of whom were customers of mine in the seed and fertilizer business. They pointed out that it would damage my reputation and my success as a businessman in the community if I proved to be the only hold-out in the community, and because of their genuine concern about my welfare they were willing to pay the dues for me.

"My response was that I had no intention of joining the organization on any basis; that I was willing to leave Plains if necessary; that the $5 dues requirement was not an important factor; and that I became quite troubled about our future."[23]

A small boycott was organized against Carter and his business. Several altercations took place; but eventually, as always happens in a well-adjusted small town, the townspeople gossiped, argued and discussed the issue until they had talked it out. For the moment. They would not agree; but they would grudgingly tolerate. They would not accept; but since they all agreed with one another anyway, how could they let such a minority opinion bother them? They would snub; they would readjust their party lists; but they must continue to live, and now they could continue to live while sharing a new bond; their disagreement with Carter's views.

Disagreements arose in small ways as well, but mostly they weren't talked about, especially between Mr. Earl and Miss Lillian. "We just never discussed our differences," says Miss Lillian.[24] Blacks went to the back of the bus; ate in separate parts of restaurants; knocked at the back door of white folks' homes. One time the son of Bishop William Johnson of the African-Methodist-Episcopal Church called to thank Miss Lillian for reaching his parents when he wanted to get ahold of them while away at school in Boston. "He was the only black man who habitually came to our front door," writes Jimmy. ". . . My daddy would leave and pretend it wasn't happening while my mother received Alvin in the front living room to discuss his educational progress and his experiences in New England."[25]

Miss Lillian recalls the first time Alvin paid a visit:

"Alvin called me when he was in the Navy. He called me from Boston, Massachusetts. We had the only telephone between Plains and Preston, the only two towns nearby. He called me and said, "I am docked here in Boston." He hadn't seen his mother in two years. "Could you possibly get her word to call me within the next few hours so I can talk to her?" So I went down to the church. It was on a Sunday. I dropped by the church and called her up, and she talked over the phone. Then, months later, he knocked on my door one Sunday night. We had a big fire and my husband was sitting by it. It seems he was listening to the radio, he had a paper, he was kind of glancing at the Sunday paper. My husband always had poor eyesight, and he always had to wear glasses and he read very little. He'd read the paper but then he'd have to rest his eyes and then read some more. You know people with bad eyes have to do that. And so this man was Alvin Johnson and I said, "Hello, Alvin." He came to bring me a box of candy for what I had done for him to get his mother on the phone, and he came in. My husband shook hands with him and went to the back of the house in our bedroom where we also had a phone, presumably to read the paper. I just stood there and talked to Alvin for a while and that is the only time he ever did come to my house. Jimmy remembers that very well. Now it is true that when Alvin's father, who was a Bishop, would come see us, we'd come talk to him at the car. In those days there was nothing like segregation, nothing like integration, it was purely . . . Well, it was just nothing except the tradition of the South."

The defense continues with a new twist: I want you to know, like I've told everyone else, that anything I did for a black, I had my husband's full support, and he paid the expenses of anything I did for the blacks. He was just as kind as I was. He didn't talk as friendly. He didn't go into the homes as I did. Then I was a nurse you see. I was still nursing sometimes. Jimmy is 51 and this was when Jimmy was a small boy. This was back, real back, when there was no such thing as integration, we didn't think about it. It was purely the black and the white.

"In fact, Alvin was here once and a reporter asked him, 'Well, what would you say about Mr. Earl?' 'Well, I would say that he was the best neighbor we ever had and anything we needed, we went to him.' Then the reporter said, 'What about this business—what Jimmy said in his book?' And Alvin said, 'That was all true. But I never did go sit down and talk to Miss Lillian.' I said, 'You can sit now.' And Alvin said, 'No, I'll just stand,' you know."

The traditions die hard.

Miss Lillian is a natural mother hen, and when her own brood was no longer around and Mr. Earl had died of cancer in 1953, she about went crazy. It was then that she took the job as housemother at Auburn University at Auburn, where she stayed for seven and a half years. Her next project was managing a nursing home for a year and a half.

In her own way, she became active in civil rights. When the Plains Baptist Church was going to decide whether or not to uphold the decision of its board of deacons to exclude blacks and civil rights agitators, there promised to be a stormy discussion. Jimmy telephoned her to warn her to stay away. "Of course, I was there early," she recalls, "because when the children tell me to do something, I usually do the opposite. There was going to be a vote on admitting Negroes to regular services, and it was pretty certain which way the vote was going to go.

"Jimmy's got a vein in his temple that throbs when he's mad, and it was really going that morning. He got up and said, 'Before we vote I've got to tell you how I feel. This is God's house, not ours. How can we stand in the doorway and tell God's people they cannot come into His house?' Seven members of the congregation—mostly Carters—voted to open the doors to everyone. About 50 voted against, but most of the people abstained, apparently because they felt as we did but were afraid of the pressures on them. For a while after the church vote there was some hostility. Not the threatening kind. Just people not speaking to each other. But faded away, just as it did when Jimmy refused to join the White Citizens Council."[26]

Miss Lillian reflects on the problems of integration: "It's just one of those deeply ingrained things. *One* person can't do anything. I do all I can."[27]

And all Miss Lillian can, is considerably more than most people contemplate, not only regarding integration but also with what to do with her life. Rarely inactive, perhaps her most famous exploit has been the manner in which, bored to tears with the petty part of small-town life, she decided to join the Peace Corps at the age of 68 and put her skills as a nurse to still further use.

Sitting at home watching the Jack Paar show on late-night television, she noticed the filler plug for the governmental organization, and with the Peace Corps log, the tag line: AGE IS NO BARRIER. That night she sent for an application, and the next day she went to Billy and Jimmy to tell them of her plans; " 'Do y'all love me?' They always know if I say that I want them to stop everything and come mow the lawn. And Jimmy says, 'Yeah,' And Billy says, 'What in the hell do you want to do now, Mama?' That's the difference in the two. And I said, 'I'm going to join the Peace Corps.' " (The reactions of the other children were also typical. Replied Gloria: "Mama, who'll go fishin' with me?" while Ruth got out her globe and said, "Oh, Mother, please try to get to Bombay 'cause I'm dying to do and I'll come visit you next summer.")[28]

"On my application I didn't even put down that I was a nurse," says Miss Lillian. "I never indicated that I was a nurse because I went in with 79, 78 others and I was the only one that was a nurse. I had nursed for 45 years. I went into family planning. We hadn't any doctors, but there were young lawyers, schoolteachers, and people like that. Young men who wanted to get out of the draft, that's who went."

During her training and preparation period in Chicago, she was always afraid that she might be told that she couldn't go. Others were getting refusal slips daily. But she persevered. "You understand you have to be perfectly healthy mentally as well as physically to get in the Peace Corps. We all had to undergo psychiatric testing, and it bothered the psychiatrists that I couldn't explain my determination to serve in India. Finally, one of the psychiatrists asked, 'Mrs. Carter, are you a liberal?' When I said I was, he explained that it was my frustrations about the plight of black people in my tight little world at home—and my inability to do very much about it—that was drawing me toward India, where I thought I could be more effective."[29]

And so, the Southern matriarch learned the Marathi dialect and went to India. Mrs. Aloo Mowdawalla, who supervises the clinic in Vickhroli (outside Bombay), where Lillian Carter performed her service, remembers her arrival in 1966: "She was very outgoing and full of zest, and wanted to make friends with everyone. . . . When my husband and I took her to the beach on weekends, or into Bombay for shopping, Lily would go out of her way to talk to people."[30]

During her first three months, she assisted on a birth control project: ". . . I did a lot of family-planning work and had to explain to those poor people why it was necessary for them. . . . If a man had more than three children, he had to have a vasectomy, which was fair. It was the only way to handle it, because those people are ignorant and the only outlet they have is sex. . . . I listened to one of the women at the clinic explained to one of the men why he needed a vasectomy: I have seen some of the men almost lose their minds. You know, they could not believe that if they had the operation they would still be men, so I would see a lot of scenes of broken men. ... I would see some of the attendants holding men down on the tables for their operation and I said, I can do better than that, so I must tell you what I did; I would stand at the man's head: he hadn't had a shot or anything, he had to stand it without anesthesia. I stood at his head and I got a pan of cold water and I would talk in a low, soothing voice and put rags on his head, and I would say, That's all right—I had a few words of Hindi that I could say to keep him calm. ... It hurts, you have to cut the thing in two and, oh, that hurts. So that's what I did with the vasectomies."[31]

Miss Lillian's most painful experience was giving a vasectomy to the father of two boys, only to see the boys die in a smallpox epidemic three weeks later. "Over there unless you have boys, you're nothing," she says. "They're very strong in that belief. And I saw that man just almost lose his mind." As a result of such experiences, she would advise the women to have their tubes tied, instead of having the men undergo vasectomies. And, after a time, she transferred to the clinic, where she gave injections and dressed wounds. When she first arrived, her supervising doctor "thought I was a C.I.A. agent."[32]

She found the caste system still in force, despite official proclaimers to the contrary (the doctor was even shocked when she once picked up his bag for him and carried it to his car); she became convinced that "the things we send them never get to the poor. They're divided among the big shots in the government. The milk, and everything"; and she tried to overcome cultural barriers through friendliness: "I accepted every invitation to eat and we would always eat from communal basins."[33]

Perhaps her most difficult and impressive task was

working with the lepers. "I'll never forget the first time I saw a woman leper," she says. "I was walking down a road and heard a rustling in the weeds. A woman all covered with vermin was trying to crawl to water. The Indians walking by refused to acknowledge her. . . .

"As much as I resented the indifference of the Indian upper classes, I was frustrated and felt useless because I wasn't much better than they were. I couldn't bear the dirt, the lice, the blood and I couldn't touch the lepers. They sickened me. After I'd been there four months, a man came into the clinic one day with his 11-year-old daughter slung over his shoulder like a sack of flour. She had infectious leprosy and weighed 30 pounds. I thought, 'Oh, God, I can't touch her.'

"I told the man to put the little girl on a cot. I went back in to the doctor's office and told him I'd never be able to touch a leper. He said, 'You know leprosy isn't transmitted by touching. Try to treat her. If you can't, I'll come and do it for you.'

"I made up my mind between his office and mine that I would do it. But after the injection, I washed my hands . . . and washed them again. Then I put alcohol on them and I was feeling very ashamed. At lunch I took a bath and put on clean clothes. And I knew that wouldn't do. I had told the man to bring the child back the next day. When she came, I simply washed my hands normally. I learned to love that girl, and after several weeks of injections, she began to get better. We got her into a leprosarium, and six months later, when she came out, she put her arms around my neck and kissed me. I thought only about how happy I was."[34]

Among Miss Lillian's other experiences was trying to get drugs for the sick natives. Her favorite ploy was to flatter the drug salesmen to get their samples. She would tell the Parke-Davis salesman that she knew Mr. Parke and Mr. Davis so well that if he gave her the samples, maybe he would get a raise. She told the Lilly man that her sons went to school with Mr. Lilly's sons, "and, oh, my goodness, it was wonderful, because I soon had cabinets full of medicine samples."[35]

Finally, it was time to leave India. Her village friends walked over ten miles to the airport to bid her farewell. "I left part of my heart there," she says; and she doesn't know if she will go back: "I'd like to go back, but all my Indian friends are mad at us because we stopped sending them wheat. . . . Maybe the next president will start sending them wheat again and I can go back."[36]

There's another way that Miss Lillian's Peace Corps sojourn might affect Jimmy, as he noted in a position paper during the campaign:

> My mother, who is now 76 years old, is a registered nurse and joined the Peace Corps in 1966 at age 68. She served for two years in a remote village in India. It saddens me to know that because of job discrimination against older people in the United States, my mother's service to India would have been almost impossible in her own country.
>   —January 26, 1976[37]

Jimmy met Miss Lillian at the airport with a special present: a beige Lincoln Continental.[38] Then they went to a family feast of chocolate cake and on to another surprise: in her absence, they had restored the pond house retreat that had burned down some years before.[39] There, and in her town house on U.S. 280 she could continue to live the full life of a Southern matriarch, active variety: "I adore all kinds of sports, indoors and out. When I'm here in Plains, I do a lot of fishing in the pond out there. It's full of lovely bass. . . . I go to wrestling matches over in Columbus when somebody'll drive me. It's not all fake, as some people think. I got Jimmy 2,000-3,000 wrestling votes over there before the Georgia primary. And I love baseball. But mostly I'm a fanatic on basketball. The underdog's ahead in this game. . . ."[40]

And, of course, being a matriarch, she has not only her own brood, but those who have married into the clan. There is the local peanut farmer, Walter Spann, who married Gloria; the veterinarian Dr. Robert Stapleton, who married Ruth (they live in Fayetteville, North Carolina); and Sybil Spires, Billy Carter's childhood sweetheart and currently Miss Lillian's most constant contact: ". . . I've just grown into the habit of calling Sybil when I need anything."[41]

And, most famously, there is the First Lady: Rosalynn Smith Carter, whose mother did invisible weaving and whose father was the town mechanic. "Everything Jimmy has ever owned, she was co-partner," says Miss Lillian. "My husband owned the business and I was just his wife. But when they came home, Jimmy and I bought the business from the other children and her name was not on the deed as a partner, but immediately she was just a co-partner."[42]

And again: "I just don't get to talk to Jimmy when Rosalynn's around. But, you know, I admire her very much. She grew up here in Plains, but she didn't want Jimmy to give up his career and come back. She was enjoying Navy life, and was afraid two families would be too restrictive. I'm proud of the way she made up her mind to adapt to small town life again, never complaining and working alongside Jimmy, just as hard as the men."

Rosalynn, the shy friend of sister Ruth; Rosalynn, whose biggest thrill as a girl was the crush in Americus when *Gone With the Wind* came to town; Rosalynn, who snagged Jimmy about the age (17) that Scarlett snagged Charles Hamilton, but who is as faithful to her husband as Melanie was to Ashley Wilkes; Rosalynn, who took over the management of the business at the age of 35, and who gradually overcame her timidity in campaigning to shake thousands of hands and make thousands of speeches; Rosalynn, who has a special interest in mental health problems and plans to work on them at the national level; Rosalynn, who at the age of 40 gave birth to the nation's most favorite lemonade-stand owner, daughter Amy. This is Miss Lillian's most famous in-law, Sister Rosalynn herself in the throes of Southern matronhood and heading toward the matriarchy (if not more) that strong family women enjoy. And this is granddaughter Amy, who has lived with Miss Lillian during the long and arduous campaign, and has learned a trick or two about stealing attention and grabbing the camera.

Or, as Miss Lillian would say: "Come on in, come on in. I've had a terrible morning. The johnny overflowed."[43]

These are the refreshing ones. Those who know their place, and let others know it; those who have lived in a small town and mastered its quirks, and sometimes embodied them. They are hard-working and frugal, but they want to help others. They are colorful, sometimes madcap, but they are commonsensical and wise. The Southern matriarch and the new women of the land; they carry the responsibility willingly, naturally. Miss Lillian, Rosalynn, Amy. Three generations, each overlapping and evolving its customs and traits; and they come from Plains, Georgia.

Besides, as Miss Lillian says: "How could Jimmy ever criticize me? I'm his mama."[44]

III. Plains Way of Life

Small towns. There is nothing so quixotic, so intriguing, so exhilarating as a small town that knows its own and knows them well, a town that cradles, that loves, that brawls and forgives. The simple men and women with no false fronts, who figure a lie is more trouble than it's worth, the way it multiplies like crab grass underfoot. The town with a good church and good food, with good men who work the land and know it well. The choir that everyone belongs to, or wishes they could, or once did, that sings hymns with a meaning that gives even casual visitors a shiver; or a backyard song, sung on the porch with the old folks in rockers and the young ones on the grass, playing and teasing, and learning the words. Lemonade stands and cherry phosphates. Turtle hunting and backpacking.

It might be Umatilla, Oregon, where the Umatilla runs into the Columbia River, 180 miles east of Portland; a trading town during the time of the Lewis and Clarke Expedition; then a railroad town; and now a small town known for its potatoes. Or Eden, Wisconsin, where the ledge from Fond du Lac tapers off into a general store and post office, and the lush, rolling hills undulate into the distance. Where the Fourth of July is an occasion for prideful celebration and the keen farmer's eye seeks frugality: Watch that budget! Or Harrisville, New Hampshire, with its gleeful play mouse poised on a giant wheel of cheese at the general store on a knoll above Nabaunsit; with a converted old mill, and with lakes dotting the countryside and beckoning the youngsters from their Saturday night square dance.

Or another small town, a town lying on the red earth of Georgia. A town of 683 citizens, where catfish is on the table and peanuts are in the soil. A town where everyone knows everyone else, and knows that they can count on each other when the chips are down. A town with clocks ticking and churchbells ringing. A town like the hundreds of thousands of other small towns in America, but a town that is sending one of its citizens to be President of the United States.

> I have never claimed to be better or wiser than any other person. I think my greatest strength is that I am an ordinary man, just like all of you, one who has worked and learned and lived his family and made mistakes and tried to correct them without always succeeding.
>
> —JIMMY CARTER
> *May 28, 1976, Ohio*[1]

What is Plains, Georgia, like? What tales do its residents tell of its most prominent citizen? How are they reacting to their newfound notoriety? What was Plains in the past, and what lies ahead in the future?

In his political autobiography and statement of beliefs, *Why Not the Best?*, Carter writes, "My best and closest friend while growing up was named A.D. Davis. He now works for a saw mill and has, I believe, fourteen children."[2]

Listen to Davis, the strapping black who rode mules and horses through the woods with Carter: "We played a lot, played wrestling games together, me and him. . . . We hunted. We didn't do too much fishing. We played baseball, and we'd get us'm a team, get nine men on each side and play one another. You'd go out there and play and there'd be all the fun you'd want.

"Jimmy doesn't like to lose. But he always loved to be up front. You know, he loved that. Everything he started out with he was always good at. He's hunted a lot. He's good on hunting. He was also good on boxing. I could throw him, but I couldn't outbox him. I used to tell him that someday he'd be a boxing champion."

Expansive and relaxed, but serious, Davis revealed an episode that illustrates how Carter helped him to handle a tragic episode that could have ruined Davis's life: "I killed a man. He tried to kill me and I killed him, and I had to go to jail for manslaughter. This was about the time Jimmy was running for governor, and he told me if he got elected, he would try to help me.

"Now other people wouldn't have done that kind of business, with that responsibility. Once he talked to me while I was on a prison truck, and he didn't have to. He could a kept on like he didn't know me, but he didn't. He told me what he was gonna do and that's what he did."

Davis focused his attention on the dark episode and the details of the drinking spree that night. "Both of us were looking to be dead. That's the way it was. He stabbed me and I shot him. He thought I was going to die, too; but I didn't. We'd been drinking, both of us had been drinking—you know how things work out. If I had been sober, maybe I could have avoided it, have walked away from it. You're sorry afterward, but you can't do nothing about it. That's the way it was with me. I've wished many days I could take it back, bring it back, but I can't do it."

The experience changed Davis: "I have served the Lord ever since. I ain't got no other choice but to serve the Lord, because I promised him I'd work for him all my life. That's what I do."

Jimmy Carter's efforts to help Davis regain his sense of

self seemed natural: a friend was in trouble, and it was second nature to help him regain the right path. Second nature because Jimmy Carter isn't the first (and won't be the last) of the Carters to lend a hand. "Our children will be the sixth generation to own the same land," Carter has written.[8] The red earth of Plains is in his blood; and from it he can draw his sustenance and strength.

If the child is Father of the man, the models of a child are important in molding his character. For Jimmy Carter there was Miss Lillian—witty, intelligent, gentle and plain-speaking; and Mr. Earl, a natural sage and a man with a shrewd business sense. Joe Bacon grows reflective and tells a story on himself and Earl Carter: "I made a mistake right before the Depression and invested foolishly in cotton. I thought FDR was the second Jesus Christ, but Earl Carter knew otherwise and waited for the right time to invest his money in cotton. I have had seven children in my lifetime and am 77 years of age. My philosophy is mind your own business and leave others alone. I believe in what Thomas Jefferson said: 'The power to tax is the power to destroy.' I also agree with Ben Franklin's comments in 'Dangers of a Salaried Bureaucracy': 'Sir, there are two passions which have a powerful influence in the affairs of man. These are ambition and avarice—the love of power and the love of money.'"

Like so many unsung citizens across the United States, Earl Carter, too, could be counted on when the chips were down. P.J. Wise, owner of an electrical business in Plains and engineer for the nearby Americus and Sumter County Hospital in Americus, recalls what it was like when times weren't so good.

"Earl worked real hard during his lifetime. During the Depression I remember one evening he would come to town with patches on his britches just like everybody else. And he had concern for people. He helped lots of farmers, helped them borrow money, helped them get the farm up again when they were down and out.

"Then, too, he was always for something progressive for the community. He served on the school board for a long time, and he tried to do all he could to better schools. I reckon he was one of the first directors of the REA when it came into being, and he served well on that.

"I remember when I built my house right after World War II, they weren't going to set two poles to give me electricity and I went to Mr. Earl and told him that the manager wasn't going to run electricity over to my house." Mr. Earl took up the case and "the next day the truck drove out there to my house and was ready to put in the power. He was one to see that everybody was treated, I think, as fairly as anybody could be, and he'd go to bat for anybody he thought was right."

The businessman also recalls that once he had done some work for a man and it looked as if he would not get the $400 he was entitled to. He told Mr. Earl of his problem, and that he couldn't afford to lose that much. "And one morning I went by the post office to get my mail and there was my check. I feel sure if Mr. Earl hadn't told me he'd see about getting it that I'd never have gotten it."

John Lundy, a black, echoes Wise's sentiments about Earl Carter and extends them to other members of the Carter clan as well: "I moved to Plains in 1950. I needed insurance for my Ford and went to Mr. Earl Carter for a loan. He and Alton Carter provided me with the loan immediately. Alton Carter also furnished me with groceries over the years when I was down and out. Alton Carter also provided a loan so my daughter, Corie Sykes, could buy a house in 1973. I remember it well because Alton arranged for us to go through the First Federal Savings and Loan in Americus."

Says Alton Carter himself, Jimmy's uncle: "I like Plains because you can count on the people here when in trouble. I have run this store for 67 years and am 88 years of age. I owe my health to three things: One, I'm waiting for my first drink of liquor; two, I don't smoke; and three, I keep busy. My first wife, Anne, died in 1940. Elizabeth Jennings is my second wife. We were married in 1945. I have two sons, Don Carter, vice president of the Lexington, Kentucky, *Herald-Ledger*, and State Senator Hugh Carter, who runs the antique store in town with me. I have had five heart attacks."

Alton Carter's son, Sen. Hugh, still holds the Georgia State Senate Seat he ran for when Jimmy Carter left it to run for governor in 1966. Although Jimmy Carter lost that election, he's been winning ever since, and Sen. Hugh attributes Carter's meteoric rise in the presidential race in part to his small-town upbringing, with its emphasis on working hard and helping your neighbor; in short, on what millions of Americans across the land regard as practicing Christianity. Says Sen. Hugh: "Our fathers took us to Sunday school since we were babies. . . . And if you are a Christian, it will show in your life, and it shows in Jimmy Carter's life. It shows in his sincerity, in his smile, in his frankness, in his courtesy to people.

"And when Jimmy Carter talks to you, it grabs you, right off. You can feel the sincerity in him. And before you know it, instead of him talking to you, he'll have you talking to him, telling him about your life.

"My advice to you is this: If you don't want to vote for Jimmy Carter, if you don't want to get out and work for him, then stay away from him. Because if he talks to you, you're going to be hooked!"[4]

The meteoric rise of Carter is a model of hard work and persistence; "The Little Engine That Could" chugs to Washington.

I'm the first child in my daddy's family who ever had a chance. . . . I used to get up at four in the morning to pick peanuts. Then I'd walk three miles along the railroad track to deliver them. My house had no running water or electricity.

—JIMMY CARTER,
December, 1975, Jackson, Miss.;
talking to high school students[5]

As Carter said to his sister, Ruth Carter Stapleton, when she complained of campaign exhaustion: "Honey, I can will myself to sleep until 10:30 a.m. and get my ass beat, or I can will myself to get up at 6 a.m. and become president."[6] Adds sister-in-law Mrs. Billy Carter: "I like Plains because the people here consider your problems as theirs and theirs as yours. If you are married to a Carter, you never give up."

In a campaign, one man can but do his best. He needs the help of thousands of others—and help is one thing small-town men and women and big-city citizens with a neighborly heart, know how freely to give. The astonishing victory of Jimmy Carter is more truly the victory of common citizens throughout the country who realize the value of decent virtues, common sense, and pulling together; the victory of men and women who saw in Carter a person like themselves. In Plains, the coordinator of the campaign headquarters was Mrs. Maxine Reese: "I can truthfully say that nobody has turned me down on anything I asked them for. No matter what it was, weve gotten it. Now that's a big thing, 'cause you don't know how many little things we've done . . . how many primary parties, how many welcome homes at two o'clock in the morning, and the people need to go to work the next morning. I tell them 'You can sleep next year, Jimmy's coming home tonight.' And there they stood, and everybody was happy. They'd bring food and everyobdy would help do manual labor. We just cleaned the town before a barbecue. Washed it down with a water hose."

This was the spirit that elected Carter. It existed throughout the land, from Diamond Head to the Statue of Liberty, but perhaps no where so strongly as in the Old Confederacy, so long slighted since the War Between the States. A Southern parent voting for Carter was a Southern parent voting for the chance for their son or daughter to become President. For blacks and whites alike, it was a chance to rejoin the entire United States, to salve the wounds of the War Between the States in the bicentennial year of 1976. No longer was it a culture "gone with the wind"; now it was the New South, the animated South, the affirmative South. Arthur Cheokas of Americus sensed the new challenge: "I served champagne and Chablis at the October 2nd fund-raising party at the Pond House where Miss Lillian lives during the summer just outside Plains. Jimmy Carter is good for America in that Southern human resources have not often been used in our nation. How many Fortune 500 companies employ a chief executive officer who comes from the South?"

The myths of an Old South of plantations and cotton are only beginning to die. Why have Northerners so long clung to the mythic world of Erskine Caldwell and Tennessee Williams? "Those people have not come down here to see," says Plains businessman C.L. Walters, Jr. "Ask people who have come to Plains what they thought about the South. We got people from New York—a fellow from Americus, but now he lives in New York—who said that everybody he met up there said they had never been out of New York. They thought everybody down here lived in plantation homes and had people in the fields. You're either a slave or you're a wealthy landowner. And they just don't know 'cause they've never been down here."

Walters himself has moved around and lived in larger cities like Atlanta and Savannah, Jacksonville and Montgomery; but he grew weary of traveling, and he wanted one thing: roots. "I just got tired of moving around. When kids grow up I want them to know that they're coming to a certain location for Christmas, not Atlanta one year and Charlotte, North Carolina, the next year, and so forth.

"'Roots' is what I mean, and also there's a certain amount of security in a small town. If something happens to you, you're gonna be taken care of. You don't have to go to the city or the state of country and ask for assistance because somebody's in the hospital bleeding. You know your neighbors will help you.

"The house I live in now is my grandmother's house. It's been in our family since '32 or '33. My mother is talking now about leaving her house to us because one of my kids might want it, rather than selling it when she dies. We just bought a small house, a three-room house, which belonged to my great-grandfather here in Plains and had it moved to our lot."

Walters grew reflective about his experiences in the outside world: "I believe honestly that 80 per cent of the people in this country would move to a small town if they could make the money they're making in a small town. You go out in your back yard and you holler; the neighbors don't scream—they don't pound on their walls at you. It's the lifestyle in a small town. I've got a college degree and it's done me a little good. It's taught me to do what I thought I wanted to do."

Walters' wife, Sandra, echoed his realization that some human priorities can't be bought: "My children have an individuality here in Plains that is not there in a city life. You must care what people think in a small town. Most people want their children to grow up in an atmosphere where people care and yet still have the conveniences. Too many children today hang loose after graduating from college. As a result, they are having a difficult time in coping with the realities of life. There is so much more in life than money. I supported my husband's education while he was at Georgia Tech. He then worked as a technical engineer in Atlanta, Jacksonville, and Montgomery. Fed up with this nomadic existence, he said, 'Let's return to Plains and open a grocery store.' I have three children: Craig, 7; Carol, 10; and Cathy, 13."

What is the philosophy of a family like Walters'? Says C.L.: "Well, I try to do several things. One is to serve God—this is not corny, everybody in town feels pretty much the same way and we're not overdoing it just because of the Carters. It's always been here."

Does Carter dramatize or magnify this feeling?

"Well, no, not really. It's just that people have just noticed it because he's saying it nationwide. We don't go out and preach it on the street corner, but we try to live it in such a way that sets an example for others. And also, very strong family ties. We are all very sorrowful if somebody else's child gets in trouble. My heart would be broken if one of my close friends' child got in trouble as much as it would be my own, just about. And I believe strongly in church ties and family ties. And that's something that you lose in the city. But it's something that if you live in a small town and you don't have it, you're not happy."

I am a businessman and a Christian. I am a father and a Christian. I am a politician and a Christian. I am a governor and a Christian.

I have been a better businessman, father politician and governor than I am a Christian, because in my secular positions I have never been satisfied with mediocrity. I am, at best, a mediocre Christian. It is obvious that in these present times, as Christians we need to recognize frankly our own inadequacies and

failures, ask God's forgiveness, and commit ourselves
to a standard of perfection.

—JIMMY CARTER,
May 11, 1974, Detroit;
speech to Christian
Businessmen's Committee[7]

The church is the bedrock of the small-town community, and its praise is to the Lord. When the churchbells
ring in Plains, the congregations assemble in the six
churches, three white and three black, and contemplate
how to follow in the path of righteousness for His name's
sake. All across the land, the common men and women
gather in a most uncommon manner. They know that
something, somewhere is larger and more important than
they; and they gather to contemplate that special
presence.

The Rev. Bruce Edwards, pastor of Plains Baptist
Church, to which the Carters belong, says that he has
served other churches in the area and that "I don't feel it
to be a whole lot different at all. It was a rural-like setting
I was in before and this is a small-town type setting and
the people are basically the same. . . . By and large where
I have lived—Jacksonville, Florida, New Orleans, Americus, and now Plains—people are roughly the same. In a
small-town situation you have a closer identification with
people than you do in the larger metropolitan areas.

"I think people here are closer. This may be primarily
because a good many of them are closely related physically. Brothers and sisters, aunts and uncles. The town of
Plains is made up primarily of the Williams, Carters,
Dodsons, and a few other families. But still all of them
are kind of interrelated in some way or another. So this
may account for some of the close identification people
have with one another.

"I do think our people are deeply religious people. If

there's something that means something to them, it's not something they just intellectually believe with their minds, but it's something that governs the way they live."

Soren Kierkegaard, Paul Tillich, and other famous theologians may at times crowd Jimmy Carter's reading stand; but it is Rev. Edwards with whom he comes into most constant, direct contact. During the campaign, opponents attempted to turn Carter's true religious beliefs into a sham by chiding him for giving an interview to *Playboy* magazine.

Commented Rev. Edwards on Carter and the interview:

> "I have been tremendously impressed by the depth of his faith and how it does affect his own personal life. I think the truthfulness of those statements in the *Playboy* magazine interview is an indication of how deep his religious faith really is instead of how shallow it is, as some people would challenge. I think if you looked beyond the fact that this was in *Playboy* magazine and beyond the colloquialisms that he used, he had some very deep theological thoughts about the way he views other people, that most people would do well to practice. This has impressed me. . . ."

Another episode at the church impressed the nation: On Sunday October 31, 1976, two days before the November 2 election, a black minister named Clennon King arrived at the church to find its doors closed to him. Services had been cancelled, and Rev. Edwards, acting at the direction of the church deacons, refused Rev. King entrance. In the 1960's eleven of the twelve church deacons—and the pastor—voted to exclude blacks. Carter was the twelfth deacon and had missed the important deacons' meeting. His only chance to change the church policy was to persuade the monthly church conference to reverse the decision of the deacons' meeting. He had to get up extra early and drive from Atlanta to be able to be at the meeting, but he did it; and he pleaded for an open policy. In the next decade, he was pleading again; and this time, after the election, in the bicentennial year of 1976, the Plains Baptist Church opened its doors to blacks.

About Carter's position before this occurred, Frank (Nub) Chappell, Jr., a lifelong friend of Jimmy Carter's, states: "I don't know if it was any big deal, what he did. But he had guts enough to get up and say it anyway, which took a lot at the time. You know what I mean. When the situation is such that it was the way it was, people did a lot of things they're ashamed of during those times."

When asked why he didn't quit the church after it had refused to let Rev. King worship there, Carter said that if the human race was not perfect, he would nevertheless not resign from it; and if his church had flaws, it would be better for him to work from within than to quit. An earlier comment on June 13, 1974, at the Southern Baptist Convention in Dallas, Texas, indicates how this attitude might affect his approach to the standards of government:

> The standards of government should exemplify the highest attributes of mankind, and not the lowest common denominator. There is no legitimate reason for different standards in our home, our office, our church, or our government. In every component of life we should continually strive for perfection as commanded by God.[8]

So, the church endures; and so does the humanity of Plains. A.D. Davis, Carter's black boyhood friend: "The people are friendly. They share with you. You get in a tight, you can go to 'em, and say let me have such and such a thing and maybe I'll pay it back to you one day, and they'll let you have it. That's the reason I say this is the place to be. It's the only way to get something when you ain't got nothing."

Charles Hicks, who has lived within five miles of Plains all his life, describes the general atmosphere: "It's a place where, if you respect yourself, you can sure be respected and get help. First of all you've got to make your step. And if you're honest and sincere, then you'll get help. I like the people around here."

Mill Simmons gives the opinion of a nearby outsider and a slant on how a town like Plains relates to its neighbors: "I am an insurance agent in Americus. People like people in Plains. We have friendly competition here. For example, Jan Williams of the Williams' peanut family handled all correspondence for Lillian Carter during the campaign at no expense. Also, I like Plains because I can hunt dove, quail, and deer within two miles of town."

Perhaps more rambunctious and seemingly less typical of the Plains way of life is Billy Carter, the outspoken, bespectacled brother of Jimmy Carter, who Jimmy once said "reads almost as much as I do." Although he has managed the peanut business and turned it into a multi-million dollar venture, Billy would as likely be seen in "Billy Carter's Service Station," where he dispenses free booze on Sundays (to avoid the prohibition of Sunday liquor sales), as at the Carter Warehouse. Open and cheerful, with a creased redneck and a cussing vocabulary, he has a theatrical flair that is the treat of national media looking for off-beat copy.

When he lost the race for mayor of Plains by a few votes, despite running on a platform of keeping Plains as much like it was as possible, rather than to let fly-by-night business ventures open, he tersely commented that for all he cared "Plains can go to hell." He makes a colorful sibling; and when he lost, Miss Lillian graciously commented that Billy was still much more interesting than Jimmy.

Early on the night of the first debate between then-President Gerald Ford and Jimmy Carter, a member of the national media ignored the No Trespassing sign outfront of the Carter Warehouse, and asked him if he was going to watch the confrontation. "I couldn't be less interested," he deadpanned. "I probably won't even look at the thing. I'm tired and I want to go to bed."

Small wonder. On a typical day Billy is at work early, and during peanut season in the fall, he may work until midnight. Ordinarily he is a light sleeper, rarely getting more than a few hours sleep at night: "I may go to bed early and then get up at 1:00 or 2:00 a.m. and read for the rest of the night."

If he doesn't have a can of beer in hand, then it's a cigarette; and he once revealed that he smoked four or five packages a day, many of them while reading in the predawn hours. He prefers to wear the casual dress or work clothes of Plains and is emphatic about not having to wear a tie unless absolutely necessary, a style that downplays his success as an entrepreneur. And when he's not at the Carter Warehouse, he's across the street at the simple service station, where he drinks and jaws with his cronies, and where the tourists now ask and receive his autograph. So popular, unpredictable, and colorful has he become in his media appearances, that he has been asked to appear on many television shows as well as to give countless interviews.

Billy's not alone. Sen. Hugh reports that tourists are interested in meeting anyone with the Carter name and often as not will ask for an autograph on being introduced. "I have more business than I can handle at my antique business," he says. "I don't want any more at this time."

Sen. Hugh says he spends most of his time talking to members of the press and other media people who have come to Plains to do stories on the new president, and that he has done this at the request of the president.

"I remember that my wife and I were alone at home one Sunday while Jimmy was still governor. He knocked on my door and entered. He was dressed in sneakers and blue jeans.

"He told us that he had something to tell us and wanted us to be among the first to know. He then told us that he was going to run for President of the United States.

"We were very surprised, of course, and asked him why.

"He said that a number of persons being mentioned at that time as potential presidential contenders had visited him at the Governor's Mansion, or he had met them elsewhere.

" 'After talking with them and getting to know them, I believe that I am as qualified to run as any of them. And if we can be successful in letting the people know that I am as smart as anyone, I think we can capture the presidency,' said then-Governor Carter."

Sen. Hugh agreed that Jimmy could win, and told him he would be pleased to help him anyway that he wanted.

"It was then that Jimmy told me that he wanted me to look after the home front by meeting with the press and telling them what they wanted to know about the candidate." His interviews run into the hundreds and are time-consuming, but Sen. Hugh is proud to be able to help his cousin.

He also reveals how his church has been taxed by the crowds of tourists joining regular worshipers: "We are always filled to capacity and have sometimes turned away three to four hundred persons. The people come, of course, because they know that if Jimmy is in town he will attend the Sunday morning service.

"We lock the doors of the sanctuary to allow those regular attenders in Sunday School to get seats, then we unlock them and let people sit as long as there is room. Some of the people have caught on, however, and come to Sunday School to make sure they can obtain seats."

Indeed, the Plains way of life has changed appreciably since the spring of 1976 because of the large number of tourists who wanted to see what Jimmy Carter's hometown was like. In an eight month period more than 50,000 persons registered as guests in the town depot, and there were, of course, many others who were not registered.

The high priestess of Plains and manager of Carter's Plains campaign headquarters, Mrs. Maxine Reese, notes how well the townspeople have held up under the stress: "Fortunately, so far we've taken it in with good humor. And as you say, we are proud, very proud. And my whole idea the whole time was to put on the best face, to be happy, to be nice to people. I think the town has done a good job so far."

Typical of how Plains citizens feel about the invasion by outsiders, Mrs. Reese says: "This is something we don't have any prior experience about, and we don't know. The only thing I know, and that I have found out, is that if you're nice to someone, they're not gonna be all bad."

As to any changes in Plains, Mrs. Reese states that "the city limits of Plains are going to remain constant. They're going to strive to control what's inside. Whatever is built will have to be built outside the city limits. The city limits of Plains go in all four directions exactly one-half mile from the depot. The depot's in the center of town, and was built in 1888. Plains has not always been near the railroad. At one time it was about a half mile out 45. But when the railroad came, Plains just moved in to the railroad."

Mrs. Reese continues: "What I'm trying to say, is that

plans are under way to try to control what happens in Plains. We're hoping the motels will continue to stay in Americus. Let them build all they want. It's not but nine miles. In a city you don't think about driving across town."

But despite the efforts of Plains to stay the same, each morning carloads of curious tourists inundate the town. Every parking area is filled; stores are swamped with purchasers of souvenir items; and visitors swarm about the Plains Baptist Church, hoping to catch a glimpse of its most famous Sunday School teacher. A new restaurant called "The Back Porch" has opened, along with various other stores, most of which primarily sell items that can be used as souvenirs.

Boze Godwin is one of those businessmen of Plains who has mixed emotions about what has transpired in Plains during the past few months. He readily concedes that he is in favor of "anything that is for the betterment of Plains," but hates to see any of the old features lost. With others, he supports the long-range plans designed to help Plains control its growth rate.

What is there about living in Plains that means so much?

"In the past it meant a way of life, a slow, easy pace, a good lifestyle," says Godwin.

"We have an opportunity to make more money, that's true, but I still want things to be the way they once were, and I want my children to live in that sort of environment also."

One thing the presidential change has brought for Godwin is that it means a lot more work to make the increased funds he is speaking about. On a Saturday or Sunday, the town of 683 residents may play host to as many as 2,000 tourists.

"I used to be open only 5½ days a week," says Godwin, who is the third generation pharmacist with his business site located in the same building. "Now I find that I have to be open Wednesday afternoon and Sundays as well because of the large number of tourists."

If he had a choice of having it like it was in the past or now, which would it be for Godwin?

"I'd like it to be like it was, I think. That's a hard question to answer because I have been able to make more money the way it is now."

And how *was* Plains? Where did it come from? What is its history before Jimmy Carter put it on the map of the nation's minds? What was it like back then?

The first settlers were Creek Indians, who were displaced in the year 1827 under the auspices of the Treaty of Washington. As early as 1840, whites and blacks were moving into the area. Three separate settlements were quickly established, including Plains of Dura, Magnolia Springs, and a third near Lebanon Cemetery. In 1885, the first railroad ran through Plains of Dura; and the residents decided to shorten its name simply to Plains. The charter for the Town of Plains was adopted on December 17, 1896. In January of the following year, the town elected its first mayor and four city councilmen: Dr. B.T. Wise, mayor; and R.S. Oliver, W.L. Thomas, L.D. Wise, and E. Timmerman, Sr., councilmen.

H.L. Hudson built the first house ever constructed in Plains, one currently owned by Mrs. Mozell Mize. He was the first railroad agent, the first postmaster, and the father of the first person born in Plains, Mary Hudson Campbell. In addition, he is listed as having donated the acreage used to build the town, including the land for the train depot.

Little did Mr. Hudson know that generations later the depot had halted operations because of lack of passenger service. And even more unbelievable to him probably would be the use of that same structure to house the campaign headquarters for a presidential winner from his own town of Plains.

About 1910, after the initial telephone exchange had started, the business section of Plains was completed. It was from around this time that older residents, such as Joe Bacon, remember the Carters. He describes being hit by a wet flying object thrown by one of the family members in those early years: "It was the first time I was ever hit by a snowball."

The oldest resident of Plains is Miss Nell Walters, 93, who has lived in the town since about 1913: "I'm the oldest person born and raised here around Plains. I had a friend—he and I were the two oldest people. But he died about two months ago, so I'm the oldest person that I know of."

What of Julia Hicks, a Plains black woman, who says she is five years older than Miss Walters?

"She's not older than I am. Julia's got her age mixed up. I've known Julia since she was a child. She claims that she's that old, but I don't think she is. I know she's not older than I am because they lived on our place when she was a child and I was a good-sized girl.

"In the 1880's," Miss Walters continues, "there were only two wooden stores downtown and about four houses that I remember as a child. . . . Plains had grown a lot." She has known Carters in Plains since about 1910.

Plains gradually evolved into a busy agricultural town; and by the 1920's, it was akin to a boom town. The population was 600, almost as many as the 683 recorded as currently residing in Plains. Records show that a $50,000 bond issue was approved for erection of a new school that would accomodate at least 300 students.

There was a two-story hotel operating in the business district; and during this time the Wise Sanitarium was built at a cost of roughly $75,000. The medical facility was reportedly among the best equipped and best staffed in the nation from the standpoint of size.

P.J. Wise tells what it was like back then: "I guess like every boy I was part of some of the mischief that went on at swimmin' pools, that took place at ball games, and things of this nature that were of interest in Plains." (The town law books of that time contain a number of ordinances stating that it was illegal to be caught shooting a bow and arrow, slingshot, or any type of firearm inside the city limits.)

"My family's been here for a long time," says Wise, "and Plains is just a good place if you want to be accepted here to enjoy a good, comfortable life. The thing about Plains that people don't realize is we don't all of us agree with everything that each one of us do or say during our lifetime, but this is a place where if one of us gets into trouble, we don't have to worry about him because the rest of the community will come to your rescue. They let little bipartisan things pass by and don't even try to use it when you're in trouble or anybody else gets in trouble.

"It doesn't make any difference whether it's black or white, or anything else, because the community's always gotten along good with everybody, with the races and everything else. We've never had any problems or anything of that nature.

"I was raised on a farm. All the black boys and I went swimming together and played together and camped out at night together and everything else. We've always tried not to have any hard feelings about anybody or anything of that nature. Everybody respects one another for what they are and then they work together on different projects, and they get together and do most anything they want to, achieve most any goal that they want to, and they try to keep everybody healthy in the community and see that the needs are attended to. You just don't go everywhere in the world and find this."

The busy atmosphere of the town began to change in 1929, with the onslaught of the Great Depression.

My life on the farm during the Great Depression more nearly resembled farm life of fully 2,000 years ago than farm life today. . . .

During the field work season all the workers arose each morning at 4 a.m., sun time, wakened by the ringing of a large farm bell. We would go to the barn and catch the mules by lantern light, put the plow stocks, seed, fertilizer and other supplies on the wagons, and drive to the field where we would be working that day. Then we would unhook the mules from the wagon harness, hook up the plows, and wait for it to be light enough to cultivate without plowing up the crops.

When I was a small boy, I carried water in buckets to the men from a nearby spring, and filled up the seed planters and fertilizer distributors, or ran errands. Later, I was proud to plow by myself.

> —JIMMY CARTER,
> *Why Not the Best?*[9]

But times for a boy could still hold pleasure; and Carter and his black playmates "ran, swam, rode horses, drove wagons and floated on rafts together. We misbehaved together and shared the same punishments. We built and lived in the same tree houses and played cards and ate at the same table."[10]

P.J. Wise analyzes the indomitable spirit among the residents of Plains during the hard times: "We were happy. The reason we were happy is that everyone else was in the same boat. We didn't pay much attention to it. We all knew what was going on and how a family was poor. We had to have window shades made out of flour sacks and one year I went to school, I didn't even have a pair of shoes.

"We had plenty to eat, we were raised on a farm. We were lucky. On a farm in a community during a depression you do eat, you don't have everything you want. We used to take eggs to town, swap it for sugar and stuff. It wasn't bad."

One of the reasons no one went hungry was due to the resourcefulness of the Plains residents and the Beef Club which they formed. Under the membership plan, the families who belonged would share a cow when it was butchered to make certain that they would have fresh meat.

"In summertime when you didn't have refrigeration, you had no place to take care of your meat to keep it from spoiling," says Wise. "Every Saturday or even every other Saturday, one of the eight family members in the club would kill a calf or kill a beef, and then we'd divide that beef up, and we'd take it home. So we've had community projects such as this all our lives in this neighborhood."

Wise explains that when he was 10 or 12 years old, "It used to be my duty to go wherever in the community they were killing a calf that Saturday morning. It was always Saturday morning. I'd have to go and help skin the cow and cut up the cow, and then we would divide it and you'd get a different part of the cow every Saturday morning because there were eight pieces of cow we cut up. And then by doing that, everybody would get different pieces each week, so that ultimately one got a whole cow. . . .

"We enjoyed it on Saturday mornings getting together and talking and planning things for the community. People were closer together, they went to see one another. We didn't have a heap of automobiles back in those days. We did a lot of walking between neighbors, and things like this, that put us close together. And we knew more about our neighbors and they knew more about us, and this way everybody had a good feeling."

There were the small-town, pastoral times to give the youngsters a sense of community: "We had wiener roasts and ice cream parties, and hayrides. We used to have dates and get in the back end of a wagon at night and make a gallon of ice cream and ride around in the wagon and talk, and eat ice cream and have a big time."

But always there was the problem of money. Sometimes a boy would get a cow from his father. After killing and dressing it, he would borrow the family Model-T and drive throughout the community selling the meat. Some, who didn't work the peach field gathering the crop, would get peaches from the others and go throughout the community, selling them for 15 or 25 cents a peck. "It wasn't too expensive," recalls Mr. Wise. "I know I used to take in a lot for eggs and take in chickens and swap peaches for chickens and eggs. I know one time I got a bunch of bad eggs and I went to Oliver MacDonald's store and sold them. He found out about them and told me the next day, 'I can't sell those eggs you brought me' and that I'd have to bring in better eggs if I swapped something for them."

Jimmy Carter's memory of Depression finances is more hard-edged, as he writes in *Why Not the Best?*:

> During the Depression years, which happened to be the time I was growing up on the farm, the amount of labor expended compared to any sort of cash return was almost unbelievable. In the depths of the Depression, peanuts sold for as little as one cent per pound. It was "hard times," incredibly so. A farmer with his own manual labor and using a mule and mule-drawn equipment would break an acre of land, harrow at least twice, lay off rows, ap-

ply fertilizer, plant the seed, cultivate seven or eight times, plow up the peanuts, shake each vine manually and then place on a stack pole, let them cure for eight to ten weeks, haul the stack poles to the threshing machine, separate the peanuts from the vine, and carry his entire crop to market.

After all that, the average yield that low year was 700 pounds per acre, which gave him a *gross* return for all his year's work on that acre of only seven dollars! The average farmer planted about fifteen acres of this primary crop.[11]

Mr. Wise comments on Carter's financial attitudes: "He never wasted money. Jimmy hasn't been a big spender. He hasn't bought lots of expensive stuff for his family. He hasn't given his family everything he could. He hasn't taken big trips. He's stayed at home and worked and his family has saved. They work every day."

Another resident, businessman C.L. Walters, echoes Wise's opinion of Carter: "I think he's a very honest man, he works hard with what he gets, he's earned everything he's gotten because he's worked hard. He'll do a good job [as President]. He'll tell you what he thinks, he'll tell you if you're wrong. He's going to be the boss and I don't think you'll find any scandal. If you find a scandal, he'll see that those guys' heads are gonna roll."

Frank (Nub) Chappell, Jr., chimes in. His opinion of Carter? "He's straightforward. He'll tell you what the hell's what. He's a tough businessman, he's a good businessman. He'll tell you like it is, and that's it." What sort of President will Carter be? "He'd run the government with a little more business attitude than the way it's been running. He did a lot for the state of Georgia. Ford gave him hell about his policies and what he did in Georgia during his administration as governor. But, tell you what, he got some of them out of the big offices there and put them out in the field working with the people."

"You can see what sad shape our country's in when the Republicans are turning away from the mess in Washington. They're deserting their party and saying 'We Want Carter.' He seems like the man of the hour. He seems like the person we want, 'cause he's from outside Washington. They say, 'He's not a lawyer, he hasn't been in the Senate or House of Representatives.' To them he's sort of untarnished. He is the one person who can go in and do some good, and straighten up the mess, and reorganize."

These are the people of Plains, the people that know Jimmy Carter best. They have seen him in the fields, picking cotton by hand, or pulling peanuts out of the ground, shaking off the dirt, and stacking them on poles to dry; they have seen him in school, where Miss Julia Coleman, the superintendent, had him reading *War and Peace* at the age of 12; they have seen him courting and they have seen him playing; they have seen him shrewdly running a business and shrewdly running a campaign; they have seen him in church, arguing for equality for all, not just in principle, but in action; they have seen him as a child, and they have seen him as an educated adult.

A.D. Davis, Carter's best boyhood friend feels that he is a brother to Carter: "That's right, just two good friends. He'd come and see me wherever I was. When I was sent to jail, he came to the jail to see me."

Davis continues: "He always had a mind on trying to do something. He's the only one I believe who could really make it. He cares about people. I never heard him say an angry cuss word in the whole while I stayed around him. I never knew him to be in a fight."

The People of Plains. Walking barefoot in the rich earth. Digging honey out of bee trees. Working together to build a town swimming pool and tennis court. Hunting arrowheads. Following far enough behind so the dust from the car ahead doesn't dirty the windshield. Singing folksongs and square dancing. Playing a game of cards or dominoes or checkers with a neighbor. Going to a club meeting. Fishing. Getting the crops in on time, and praying the weather's good. Helping when there's trouble and celebrating when there's joy. It might be any one of thousands of small towns across the United States. This year it's Plains, Georgia, and this is the Plains way of life.

IV. The Unique Plains

Plains, Ga.

The press release from the Carter campaign headquarters at the old depot on the Seaboard Line says it all:

LOCATION: SOUTHwestern Georgia

   125 miles south of Atlanta

   110 miles north of Tallahassee, Florida

POPULATION: 683

SIZE: ½ mile radius

FOUNDED: 1886

HOUSES OF WORSHIP: AME

   Lebanon

   Lutheran

   Plains Baptist

   United Methodist

INDUSTRY:

Agriculture: crops—peanuts, corn, cotton, peaches

Other Businesses: 2 of the usual, with the singular exception of 1 drugstore

HISTORY OF RAILROAD DEPOT: Seaboard coastline trains
Freightroom of depot previously used for storage
All paint and labor contributed in April, 1976 for local
headquarters of the Jimmy Carter presidential campaign

Yes, a town like thousands of other small towns,
but distinctly different. A town steeped in the tradition of
the Old South, and of one of its most illustrious states. A
town of Georgia and of the people of Georgia. Consider
some of the special types:

Georgia Crackers

In the other 49 states crackers are crisp edible wafers
served with soup and cheese. Not so in Georgia.

In a chapter on Georgia heritage in the biography *Joel
Chandler Harris* by Paul M. Cousins, two characters are
introduced—William Tappan Thompsons' "Major Joseph
Jones of Pineville" and Harris' "William H. Sanders of
Shady Dale": "Both are typical representatives of the
uneducated but commonsensible middle class of Geor-
gians known as Georgia crackers, but in the best connota-
tion of that word."

B. Drummond Ayres, Jr., writing in the *New York
Times* called crackers a class "somewhere between Margaret Mitchell's antebellum aristocrats, with their white
columns and black mammies, and Erskine Caldwell's
trashy folk in the sharecropper's shack down at the end of
Tobacco Road, where the hard surface turns to rutted red
clay."

Delma E. Presley, a native Georgian who teaches English at Georgia Southern College in Statesboro and who
has just completed a study of the "cracker," says the
word does not have anything to do with rednecks or white

trash or the myth that the state was settled by convicts. That image comes from the fact that Georgia has had more of is share of poor folks, even before Sherman's March Through Georgia, and crackers were once the poor.

Presley says the word cracker can be traced back to the Scottish word "crack" which means "to boast." The people who settled much of Georgia were Scotch-Irish pioneers from the North Carolina and Tennessee mountains. In the eyes of the earlier settlers who came in through Savannah, those proud frontiersmen who began to take over were treated as rank outsiders and were made to scratch for everything they got. In their struggly out of the ashes of defeat Presley sees "the cracker coming out, the cocksure pride of having fought from the bottom of the top on your own. That's essential cracker." Crackers are the survivors against odds—like the fictional Rhett Butler, or the very real Jimmy Carter.

Poor White Trash

Poverty comes in at least two varieties: One is the honest poor. The other is poor white trash.

Paul M. Cousins in *Joel Chandler Harris* expresses it this way:

"The very lowest class in the economic and social scale was made up of poor whites, of whom there were two levels. In the upper level were those who owned small plots of ground but no slaves, who lived in very humble dwellings and yet managed to maintain their economic independence, but whose uncouth speech revealed their illiteracy." Although they were poor and uneducated, many were proud.

"In the lower level there were those scorned even by

the slaves as 'poor white trash' because of their indolence, addiction to drink and hand-to-mouth existence." Historian Ulrich B. Phillips described them as "listless, uncouth, shambling refugees from the world of competition."

The honest poor have a garden, raise chickens, patch their roof and mend their fences, put up food in jars, wash their laundry and dry it, sew, iron, mend, darn, and patch. Adults stay clean and keep their children clean. They are dependable and respectable and live in an honorable manner.

Poor white trash refers to people of the *Tobacco Road* variety, who are trifling, sorry, lazy people, who will not work or will not work steadily. They are too lazy to wash their clothes or themselves often enough to stay clean, even if someone gives them soap, they would not plant a garden, even if someone gave them seeds. Instead, they misspend what money they have on beer, a television set, or a souped-up car. They are content to live in filth and squalor and do not try to better themselves.

Children in the South who get any "raisin' " are raised to do the opposite of what po' white trash does.

Sample rules:

Do not get pregnant out of wedlock. ("Nice girls just don't.")

Do not pin a shoulder strap on underwear to avoid sewing it.

Do not take clothing out of the dirty clothes hamper and wear it again rather than wash it.

Do not gulp down food at the table.

Do not do tacky things like putting a milk carton on the table rather than pouring milk into the pitcher.

A Southern Belle

The words "Southern belle" conjure up an image of girls like Scarlett O'Hara and Melanie Hamilton in Margaret Mitchell's *Gone With the Wind* ("Scarlett O'Hara was not beautiful, but men seldom realized it when caught by her charm as the Tarleton twins were. . . .")[1] Melanie has a sweet smile and is sincere. Scarlett has a sweet smile when it serves her purpose, but when carrying out a scheme, she turns into a Jezebel. As *Time* magazine entitled an article about sexes in the South: "The Belle: Magnolia and Iron."

Rosalynn Carter and Betty Talmadge are cited "as examples of strong women who can appear pretty and helpless" and "the rest of the country makes the mistake of seeing those as ingrained ways of being rather than learned skills." Indeed, notes *Time:* "The Southern woman, long limned in a moonlight-and-magnolia image, is emerging as rapidly as her Northern sister, perhaps faster." Is Rosalynn Carter the "steel magnolia blossom" she has been described as being? Before the coming of the typewriter and the acceptance of jobs outside the home, the Southern woman was taught to get a man "as a meal ticket." Mothers taught their daughters, and some still do: "Don't love for money but try to love where money is."

Southern belles have changed hoopskirts for the Diane von Furstenburgs but some still practice the same little guiles by doing everything possible to look good and be charming. She has a bag of tricks she uses to entice a man: dropping her handkerchief or its equivalent; rolling her big blue or brown eyes; fluttering her eye lashes; feigning the vapors. It all works to make a man feel nine feet tall. Scarlett O'Hara created a moment of high drama when at the Twelve Oaks barbecue she made a game of deciding who she would "let" get her a piece of lemon meringue pie; she bestowed that favor as if it were a knighthood.

A Southern belle eats daintily. She lets a man open the door for her, hold her coat and chair and light her cigarette. She flirts, teases, speaks in a low, slow voice and laughs demurely.

A Southern belle copes and puts on a facade of utter and complete poise even in times of devastating inner turmoil. This she does unless the occasion demands that she take a strong stand on something. She can do so with a brutality that verges on verbally castrating a man. Lloyd Lewis, one of the biographers of General Sherman, of marching-through-Georgia infamy, wrote that "the fiery tongues of Southern women often provoked foragers to show their authority by rough language and to loot houses which might otherwise have gone unmolested."

Although she was taught, as *Time* said, to "be a lady. Be the moral conscience of the family. Let your husband protect you from the baser things of life. Do not challenge or compete with men. Be nice to everyone, regardless of your actual feelings," she was nevertheless prepared for her next responsibility: being a Southern lady.

A Southern Lady

A Southern belle gracefully becomes a Southern lady, and if she has been properly raised, she is ready. As Margaret Mitchell describes the upbringing of Scarlett's mother, Miss Ellen:

> ... If she was only fifteen years old, she was nevertheless ready for the responsibilities of the mistress

of a plantation. Before marriage, young girls must be, above all other things, sweet, gentle, beautiful and ornamental, but, after marriage, they were expected to manage households that numbered a hundred people or more, white and black, and they were trained with that in view.[2]

A Southern lady is generally more relaxed than she was as a girl, because she has gotten her man. She is the lady of a house run with dignity and dispatch, and her role is that of wife, mother, hostess, church member, club member, civic leader, and benefactor to the poor.

Even in times when there is not one cent of money in the house, she presides over the dinner table with the dignity of a queen. Southern women grow up with the belief that setting a good table comes after the cleanliness next to Godliness. Running out of food for guests, expected or unexpected, is a stigma second only to pregnancy out of wedlock. They also grow up in the belief that a white damask cloth ironed faultlessly, even if it is a luxury, is another necessity for "having our pride" whenever there are guests or for Sunday dinner.

When asked to "pour," the Southern lady puts on her best dress and pours with graciousness and nobility. The pouring of tea from a pot at an afternoon tea party is one of the things a Southern lady does best and only the town's leading Southern ladies are asked to pour.

The Southern lady dresses as stylishly as her budget allows. If her budget is tight, she finds ways to be stylish by ferreting out bargains and, if she does not sew herself, she seeks out skillful little seamstresses. Indeed, if circumstances force her to wear the same Sunday dress for years, she wears it like an ermine mantle.

She holds her head high. Even if disaster is at hand, she greets guests as a model of serenity. Above all, a

Southern lady rears her daughters to be Southern belles and her sons to be Southern gentlemen.

A Southern Gentleman

Although the definition of a Southern gentleman varies from community to community and time to time, some traits persevere. Many are molded in the old-fashioned, romantic notion that occurred to Sara Spano of the Columbus, Ga., *Ledger-Enquirer*, when she replied to the question, What is a Southern gentleman? "A man that looks like Rhett Butler and bows from the waist every time he meets me."

A Southern gentleman does not have a dress code the way boys have at a military school. Yet members of the same crowd tend to dress in as much of a uniform way as a teen-aged boy who cannot stand to feel out-of-place and would, for instance, rather die than be made to wear a suit to school when all his peers are in jeans.

George Washington and his contemporaries wore satin knee breeches, pumps with buckles, and powdered wigs. When defending their honor, they wore all but their tail coats.

The costume of a couple of generations of Southern gentlemen was revived when Col. Sanders of Kentucky Fried Chicken fame came on the scene wearing a spotless white linen suit, black shoestring tie, and broad-brimmed, white Panama hat.

A mode of dress still in some favor is that of the gray flannel suit—like the Madison Avenue "Man in a Gray Flannel Suit"—or a dark suit reserved for weddings, funerals, and other proper occasions. Tradition calls for a white shirt and black shoes, shined and not runover, or worn, at the heels. The white shirt is clean each morning and changed again if the gentleman goes out in the evening.

A Southern gentleman does not wear a cloak to throw over a mud puddle the way the Englishman Sir Walter Raleigh reportly did for Queen Elizabeth, but he does not hesitate to pick up a girl to carry her over a puddle—and when he becomes married, he traditionally carries his bride over the threshold of their new home. Of course, with the advent of more careers for women and of new courting attitudes, the more romantic aspects of the Southern gentleman, along with those of the Southern belle, are becoming more a part of the past than the present.

A new breed of young Southern gentlemen has emerged on college campuses today in reaction to the long hair, dirty jeans syndrome of the sixties. These young Southern gentlemen wear khaki trousers, button-down shirts by Brooks Brothers, shoes and belts by Gucci, and gray flannel jackets. For dressing up, they wear gray suits or three-piece black pinstrip bankers' suits; dinner jackets with black ties for dances; and camel-hair or black Chesterfield overcoats. Like their ancestors, they pride themselves on their impeccable appearance.

A Southern gentleman says "Yes, Ma'am" and "No, Ma'am" to his mother and to all other older women. He rises when a woman enters a room and tips his hat to a woman on the street. He takes his hat off when going inside.

A Southern gentleman not only opens the door for a woman, he holds her coat, lights her cigarette, fills her glass, and has her wait inside while he goes to park the car. He takes home the same girl or woman he brings to a dance. If he drinks, he can "hold his likker."

A Southern gentleman may also cuss like a sailor with his buddies, but he does not cuss in front of a lady; and if a cuss word should slip from his lips, he remembers to say "Pardon me, ma'am." That makes Ashley Wilkes in *Gone With the Wind* more a Southern gentleman than Rhett Butler who said, "Frankly, my dear, I don't give a damn."[3] But there is not a Southern woman living who would not prefer Rhett to Ashley, given a choice. Whether his father is a former preppie or has been to the state university, a private college, a fraternity, or any place known for its old school ties, he follows in those footsteps and often into his father's profession as well. In short, a Southern gentleman is a man of honor who abides by the Ten Commandments. Should he deviate, slightly or wholeheartedly, he is discreet.

At Christmastime in 1976 in Plains, Ga., someone put up an ugly green plastic Christmas tree on city property across the street from Billy Carter's service station. There were several ladies present when Billy Carter cussed the plastic blight: "Close your ears now, ladies, that is the —————Christmas tree I have ever seen in my whole life."

According to Aldo Beckman in the *Chicago Tribune*, "The station crowd broke into hee-haws, and 'the good ole boys' reached for another beer."

The Good Ole Boy

In the simplest of terms, a good ole boy is a boy you went to high school with and the person you would most like to have along when you have had a flat tire on a backroad in Georgia, and there is no spare in the trunk. He is the fellow you want along when help is needed.

Bob Poole, Washington correspondent for the *Winston-Salem Journal*, wrote in a column that after the national press discovered Billy Carter's service station in Plains, every reporter still able to prop himself up in front of a typewriter was trying for a definition of a "good ole boy." Such a definition is "as slippery as a handful of steaming grits. Prudent people know this, of course, and leave it alone."

Some people have "been fooled by Jimmy Carter's accent, work boots and love of stock car racing, and have blundered into labeling Jimmy Carter a good ole boy. Rubbish. If Jimmy Carter is a good ole boy, Richard M. Nixon is Diogenes. . . ."

Poole points out that Jimmy Carter "is too distant, humorless, pious and single-minded to qualify." Good ole boys have time to sit around and talk about topics like the weather. Chances are that when Jimmy goes to Billy Carter's service station it is not to sit around and chew the fat but to get gas, talk something over with Billy, or even to be photographed so he will look like a good ole boy."

James Taylor, an aide to Rep. Stephen L. Neal, and a noted authority on good ole boys, has brought the sexual criterion into the definition of good ole boys: "The term is confined almost entirely to the masculine. You rarely hear a woman calling a man a good ole boy."

Good ole boys are to be found in any social class. It is "a fraternity generally fragmented into what might be called stratified peer groups." But, notes Taylor, "It would be rare that you would find somebody who makes $3,000 a year calling somebody who makes $50,000 a year a good ole boy."

Other observations by Taylor:

Being a good ole boy is the Southern equivalent of charisma and denotes the highest order of acceptability among one's peers.

It is not related to age. "I've known good ole boys past 40," Taylor says. "Most of them have never really grown up."

Being designated a good ole boy has absolutely nothing

to do with character or reputation. More often, it simple means one is just "one of the boys."

Rascality is not a necessity.

A good ole boy can be virtuous but not self-righteous; temperate but not intolerant; reserved but not snobbish; loquacious but not a braggart.

One measure of good ole boyism is to be accepted by others in the fraternity. Billy Carter is so highly regarded by his peers that in the autumn of 1976 they invited him to give the keynote address at the Annual Good Ole Boys Convention in Alabama. In his modesty and, perhaps because he does not like to go anywhere that takes him from home overnight, Billy turned them down.

All these various Southern types—from Southern belle to good ole boy—lead a lifestyle that is varied and unique. To understand the South takes a lot of readin', a lot of talkin', a lot of visitin'.

"Belonging" is of major importance in the South. Robert Manson, in an article from Jimmy Carter in *New Times* gets to the heart of the matter when he quotes a Southerner:

"Asking someone where he's from and how he answers can tell you a lot about him. Now, a Northerner will say, 'Oh, from Pennsylvania, or New England' and sometimes you even hear, 'Not from anywhere in particular.' A Southerner would never say that. He would always be specific. 'Cocktaw County' he would say, narrowing down as much as he could so you would know him better and feel more at ease. And, you say, 'Boy, where does your daddy hunt?' If you say that, well, you're really down home."

Southerners have another way of placing or identifying people. Jimmy Carter has been described as a "Carter from Plains." A man is often described as "a Bankhead from Rome, Ga.," or "a Gaylord from Columbus, Ga."

Many a Southern mother when a daughter dates a stranger has been soothed by a report that "he is a Bankhead, from Rome, Ga."

The fact that Jimmy Carter is a "Carter from Plains" is identifying because Southern families did not move about as much and towns were small enough so that both families and individuals were well known. Their honor, their fidelity, and whether they pay bills is common knowledge. It has been said that in a small town people not only know if a man beats his wife but why.

All that is not to say that just because a man is a Carter or a Gaylord, that two or more brothers are alike. Certainly Jimmy Carter and his brother, Billy, have different ambitions, if nothing else. Nor does a person born into a poor family have to remain poor or put upon; many have risen out of their poverty. And scoundrels or "black sheep" are sometimes spawned in the best of families.

Belonging to a family in the South, as evidenced by the continued popularity of family reunions, has a meaning that is not possible in big cities like Pittsburgh, Los Angeles, St. Louis, or even Atlanta—cities largely populated by members of the American mobile society.

The late Latimer Watson, who for years was the Grand Dame and Society Editor, of the Columbus, Ga., *Ledger,* was well acquainted with the value of family ties and the place of Society in the South. She wrote about their doings in every edition. When Sara Spano continued the column in that paper in the current democratic manner, with emphasis on people of all kinds, names unknown to Latimer Watson began appearing. One day Latimer Watson asked Mrs. Spano, "Sara, who are these people? I don't know them." Mrs. Spano answered that if she did not "know" the people, then they at least deserved the publicity of having their names in print.

Charles Ravenel of Charleston, S.C., is not the same kind of Southerner as Jimmy Carter (he went to Harvard and made it on Wall Street before returning) yet he does understand and appreciate the South: "We have something down here. Sometimes I am not sure what it is myself, but when I look North and see all those people gobbling pills to forget their surroundings, I know that whatever it is we have down here, I want it to be my life."

New York Times columnist Russell Baker, analyzing the November 1976 election, said it this way: "In its old age, America yearns for the sticks. First, it was the children, 10 years ago, chucking it all, chucking the tailored threads and the rat race and dad's suburban martini pitcher and two cars under the phony carriage lamps, chucking the bright lights and the swarming excitement of conurbations, chucking it all to find salvation in the woods . . .

"As for the Democrats, in Carter they have chosen the most countrified of all, and in the choosing, black voters, who are the most distressed of city dwellers, went strongly for the man from the sticks."

Time called the South, "the last American arena with a special, nurtured identity, its own sometimes unfashionable regard for the soil, for family ties, for the authority of God and country. Despite the influx of outsiders, the South remains a redoubt of old American tenets, enshrined for centuries by the citizenry."

"Throughout its long and often tragic history," the *Time* article noted "the South was looked upon as an arena that endured much and learned little. Could it be that in many ways it can now teach the nation how to live? The idea can easily be exaggerated, but there is truth in it. The fact was foreshadowed by the South's agrarian romantics of the 1930's, who in a sense anticipated 'the greening of America,' the new emphasis on human values and environment.

"Later the harshly segregated South showed the rest of the nation that it was possible to change despite deeply held prejudices—and to achieve at least the beginnings of racial amity. Other parts of the United States, without consciously turning to the South, began to long for some of its values: family, community, roots."

The South has its problems; but they are not typically the problems of big government, big cities, the ills of urban living, crime in the streets, poor housing, or pollution from gas-guzzling automobiles. On Saturday afternoon in Plains, Ga., just before the election, Alton Carter, Jimmy Carter's uncle, left the safe in the back of his store wide open while he went up the street to his home. Although the influx of visitors is bringing changes, the people of Plains still felt no need to lock their doors against intruders.

This open, roamin' quality about a small town is related to the hospitality of its people; and Southern hospitality is as indigenous to the region as *Gemütlichkeit* is to a Münchener. It's a way of being and of thinking—a warmheartedness of which one is justifiably proud.

Southern hospitality

One's first reaction to defining the term is the same as that of the black woman who was asked how to cook collard greens. With a shake of the head, she said, "She don't even know how to cook collards!" Cooks are born with the recipe in their mouth, the way a Boston Brahmin starts out with a silver spoon.

Southern hospitality was in full bloom before the Civil War. Distances between plantations were so great that trips took days and when guests arrived, the custom was to make them welcome for as long as they cared to stay. The invitation "Y'awl Come" is a part of Southern hospitality because if no one came to a household, the people who lived there had to content themselves with talking only with each other.

A visit to the restored Tullie Smith House, built around 1840 and one of the few prewar homesteads still standing in the Atlanta area, is a testimony to Southern hospitality. To the left of the front porch of the house is a furnished room, the door of which was left open to welcome a weary traveler when the balance of the house was closed and the occupants were asleep.

From *The First Ladies Cook Book* we learn that after the Revolutionary War, when Mrs. George Washington, who had been a camp follower in order to be with her husband, returned with him to Mount Vernon, "their lives and their home threatened to be completely swamped with the steady flow of guests." The General himself called Mount Vernon "a well resorted tavern." He and his wife were forced into the role of the nation's hosts; but even in their unofficial capacity as private citizens, they accepted the duties with graciousness.

A review of the menu for the Mount Vernon Christmas dinner (included in the chapter on the Million Dollar Supper) indicates that most of the foods for the meal were grown on the place. Someone has said, "Southern hospitality is a lot easier when you have a smokehouse full of hams and a yard full of chickens that didn't cost any money than if you have two pork chops that cost 30 cents each in the refrigerator." (The fact that hams and chickens "didn't cost any money" refers to the fact that the feed for hogs and chickens were also raised on the place.)

Feeding the guests accounted "for many beeves, sheep, roasting pigs, and a considerable part of the 8 tons of pork sent to the smokehouse in a given year." In addition there were the quantities of flour, vegetables, milk, butter, fish, and game. Claret, Madeira and spirits were poured liberally. Even the cost of candles for overnight guests was no small item.

All of this Southern hospitality was paid for out of the pocket of George Washington "who considered this hospitality an important part of his duty to his country and that Martha had learned from him 'never to oppose her private wishes to the public will.' With Martha 'the General' always came first; her whole life was devoted to things which benefited her husband"—in the pattern, it might be added, of a Southern lady.

The people of Plains demonstrate Southern hospitality in action to a greater extent that experienced anywhere, but the process did not originate there, nor did it originate in those great days of the South before the Civil War, nor in the days of George Washington. The origin of Southern hospitality is found in the Bible, in such sentiments as these:

> And when ye reap the harvest of your land, thou shalt not wholly reap the corners of thy field, neither shalt thou gather the gleanings of thy harvest.
>
> And thou shalt not glean they vineyard, neither shalt thou gather *every* grape of the vineyard; thou shalt leave them for the poor and the stranger: I *am* the Lord your God.
>
> —LEVITICUS 19: 9-10.

Or:

> Then shall the King say unto them on his right hand, Come, ye blessed of my Father, inherit the kingdom prepared for you from the foundation of the world:
>
> For I was an hungred, and ye gave me meat: I was thirsty, and ye gave me drink: I was a stranger, and ye took me in:
>
> Naked, and ye clothed me: I was sick, and ye visited me: I was in prison, and ye came unto me.

Then shall the righteous answer him, saying, Lord, when saw we thee an hungred, and fed *thee?* or thirsty, and gave *thee* drink?

When saw we thee a stranger, and took *thee* in? or naked, and clothed *thee?*

Or when saw we thee sick, or in prison, and came unto thee?

And the King shall answer and say unto them, Verily I say unto you, Inasmuch as ye have done *it* unto one of the least of these my brethren, ye have done *it* unto me.

—MATTHEW 25:34-40.

Grammar school children sing a little song, "The more we get together, the more we get together, the happier we will be" that goes on something like the round "Row, row, row, your boat."

The people of Plains do what it says to do in the song; they get together. Getting together is a part of, and extension of, Southern hospitality. Before radios, televisions, and telephones, it was the living, present sound of the human voice that was important: people talking; people singing. Unless a person chose to be a hermit, the only way to communicate and to share in fellowship was to get together. More often than not it was over food; and when people came for a visit, they stayed awhile in order to talk and to learn new points of view.

Anne Jackson recalled in an interview that Cousin Booker Slye, who lived in her neighborhood, had the job of picking up the washin' from homes and piling it into his buggy. He took the laundry to the washerwoman and when the clean clothes were ready, he delivered them, usually in a basket reserved for that purpose, to the owners.

Picking up and delivering laundry was not his only function, but his life was hardly dull. He was like a honey bee as he gathered bits of news and gossip along the way and shared it at the next stop. If a person were sick, or a baby were due, the carrier was able to carry the latest information all over town.

"We miss it," Anne said. "We don't communicate that way today. Nothing beats eyeballing when it comes to communicating."

The people of Plains still work on occasions of getting together. Favorite group activities include the all-day meetin', dinner on the grounds, church suppers, family reunions, church socials, ice cream making, ice cream suppers, fish fries, barbecues, Sunday school picnics, hay rides, wiener roasts, watermelon cuttin', pitchin' horseshoes, and ball games.

Getting together when there is a death in the family is anything but a favorite activity but it has its joyous aspects because it is a time when all the kissin' cousins gather and the conversation centers on who belongs to whom and who favors or resembles whom. Knee-deep fellowship helps take the edge off a loss. A native living in New York who returned to Plains for a funeral commented on the abundant food and fellowship at the gathering: "New York cocktail parties are deadly compared to this—they never have enough food, and what they have ain't fittin' to eat."

But one place where there is something fittin' to eat is at a Southern barbecue. If you don't know barbecue, you will never understand the South. Barbecue is such a way of life that no Southern politician would dare to think he could get elected without eating barbecue.

Take former President Johnson's barbecues. Any number of writers have said that if you don't understand LBJ's barbecues, you don't understand LBJ. The meat for LBJ's barbecues was beef. The meat for the barbecues of Plains and of the rest of Georgia is pork.

The barbecue staged in *Gone With the Wind* was conducted about the way it has been for generations:

> The barbecue pits, which had been slowly burning since last night, would now be long troughs of rose-red embers, with the meats turning on spits above them and the juices trickling down and hissing into the coals. . . .
>
> The long trestled picnic tables, covered with the finest of the Wilkeses' linen, always stood under the thickest shade, with backless benches on either side; and chairs, hassocks and cushions from the house were scattered about the glade for those who did not fancy the benches. At a distance great enough to keep the smoke away from the guests were the long pits where the meats cooked and the huge iron wash-pots from which the succulent odors of barbecue sauce and Brunswick stew floated. . . .[4]

Serious business, such as a decision about entering the Civil War, electing a governor, senator, or president, is plotted, planned and all but executed over plates of barbecue. Southern belles, even before Scarlet O'Hara, seized upon the occasion of a barbecue as a social setting for the purpose of meeting, sizing up and attracting a beau.

Another social get-together is the square dance. Of course, there is square dancing all over the country, especially in small towns, and each state has its square dance associations (in fact, California has had its 25th state square dancing convention; Georgia only its 4th), but it has been a while since a president loved to square-dance.

Square dance caller John Adams described square-dancing in Plains on "Satdee," October 30, 1976, the weekend before the election: "This is Western square-dancing, really. They use four couples in a square, and they do intricate moves that are called by the caller. You go to classes, and you learn fifty to seventy-five basic calls—left allamand, right, left, grand promenade and all that. Then the caller tells you what to do. Modern square-dancing is a light, fun, family affair. There's no drinking, before or during. You've got to keep fit for dancing."

The Georgia State Square Dancing Association staged the gala event in Plains. It was scheduled to take place in conjunction with a trade fair, but became absorbed by the political race. Although at first glance it seemed to be a publicity stunt, a few minutes of mingling with the crowd banished that notion. People from all over the southern part of Georgia had put on their square-dancing costumes, piled into cars and buses, and headed to Plains to dance in the streets.

From Martinez, Ga., came Kathryn and Don Greer, members of a group called the "Flutter Wheels." She wore a bright green costume with an overlay of white lace; he had on a green vest and a bejeweled tie.

The skirts of the ladies in another group were made of brown and tan gores with a brown appliqué design of a couple sitting on a fence. The dresses represented hours of needlework, but they represented something else as well: the desire to belong. If you belong, for example, to the "Peanut Twirlers," so named because a squirrel once threw peanuts at a square dance caller, you "belong" the way you belong to the Carter family or Williams family or Hicks family or the high school class of '74.

"It's my first trip to Plains," said Mrs. Shirley Byrd of Gainesville, Ga., as chicly turned out as if she were in the Beautiful People section. "Ah didn't know it would be as plain as they said it was. It's just like it was on television."

While the elders square-danced, the youngsters had

their own fun by clogging, a dance in which heavy shoes, or clogs, are worn for hammering out a lively rhythm. Stalks of sugar cane were sold (thirty-five cents for two stalks). Babies in strollers watched wide-eyed from the sidewalks. No admission or minimum was charged, so that the dancers in Plains danced to their heart's content, and as long as their bodies could, for free. Here was inexpensive, exhilarating fun for the whole family—"Satdee nite" in Plains.

A free square dance is not necessarily unusual in a town like Plains. People are used to making their money go far, and to figuring out ways to enjoy life that don't require undue expense. "Although we didn't have a lot of money," says Rosalynn Carter, "I was never concerned about it." Families would swap produce and their own skills. A. D. Davis, Jimmy Carter's childhood playmate, remembers that during hard times his take-home pay wouldn't be as much as $25 a week; but the general word during that time, the time of the Depression and up until World War II was "we didn't have any money, but neither did anybody else. We were poor but we didn't know it. We just had a grand time growing up. We had our pride." Miss Lillian, in fact, pooh poohs the idea that the Carters were poor, although Jimmy writes as much in *Why Not the Best?* Her attitude seems to be similar to that of Martha Washington, who said that "the greater part of our happiness or misery depends upon our dispositions and not our circumstances."

And Plains residents like the Carters knew how to make do with what was at hand, and with the goods and services of their neighbors. Sometimes it was a cashless society because somebody didn't have any cash. When Miss Lillian nursed a young girl who had diphtheria, she didn't expect to get paid, "at least not in cash," as Jimmy writes in *Why Not the Best?*:

... The girl's parents were very poor. Eventually she died and a few weeks later the girl's father drove into our yard with a one-horse wagon loaded down with turpentine chips. He had traveled more than a day to get there.

Although the wood chips had little monetary value, they were extremely helpful to use because they burst instantly into a roaring flame when touched with a match and were useful in starting a fire in the stove or fireplace, an early morning necessity for us. I remember that we unloaded the turpentine chips into a pit used for storing ferns and flowers during the winter, and we benefited from their use for several years.[5]

The use of turpentine chips to aid in warming the house brings to mind a lifestyle involving wood instead of gas or electricity, and Jimmy Carter's boyhood: "We lived in a wooden clapboard house alongside the dirt road which leads from Savannah to Columbus, Georgia, a house cool in the summer and cold in the winter."[6] The fireplace of his early years served not only as a source of heat to cook food and to warm the house, but also as a source of light for reading.

An area near the house was used for the wood pile. Often there was a woodshed for storing cut logs and also kindlin', those thin strips of wood that make it easier to start a fire. To give someone "a wood shampoo" meant to hit them over the head with a stick of wood. The logs for the wood came from cutting down trees "on the place" by hand. The logs were cut into shorter lengths by the cross-cut saw powered by a kerosene motor; the shorter lengths, especially, were split with an ax. The motorized saw was a luxury not all farms could afford, and there were men who went from house to house cutting wood in exchange for various specialities of the house. If they were working around dinner time, they were naturally welcomed into the house to eat.

Jimmy Carter has written that sawing wood was one of the "continuing" burdens of farmlife before the coming of electricity. A boy who was supposed to keep a constant stack of stove wood and kindlin' but failed, knew such failure could assure a whippin'. Boys in a household were assigned the duty of "totin' " wood and kindlin' into the kitchen where it was placed in a wood box.

In an unwritten priority system, if the boys had to help with work on the farm in busy seasons or help with the stock (the animals), the cook or even the lady of the house carried in wood and kindlin'.

Each woodpile had a chopping block cut from a hefty log. It was about two feet high and served the same purpose as the fancy chopping block now available for modern kitchens. The chopping block was used primarily as the base on which a smaller log was placed so it could be chopped by an ax. But it also served as a base for cracking nuts and for various culinary purposes. For example, cooks inept at wringing the necks of chickens, often found it useful to place the neck on the chopping block and use an ax.

Experiences with the woodpile and barn are part of life on the traditional farmstead. Dr. Bergen Evans, who in 1972 completed 41 years of lecturing at Northwestern University in Chicago, said in a speech that when he was growing up, the woodpile and barn were places to go—to work, to play, or to meditate. They are now among the haunts lacking for today's youth; but for Jimmy Carter, a barn loft was a place from which to jump into "huge piles of oat straw," a treat not in the catalog of F.A.O. Schwartz.

Wood from the woodpile was used not only in the fireplace but also in a wood stove consisting of the following parts: a fire box where the fire is built; an oven; four or more surface units each covered with an iron "eye" that rests flush with the surface of the stove; and a "warmer" or chest up over the surface that was kept warm by the heat from the stove and from the flue, which was, of course, the duct that allowed the passage of smoke up the chimney. Appropriate leftovers were stored in the warmer, where children home from school also found such luscious snacks as fried peach pies.

To today's homemaker, the wood stove might appear as bewildering as a steam boiler plant, for to operate it properly requires intuition and a touch of kitchen genius. The stove has no thermostat, no push button control. Although there is a gauge in the oven door that indicates whether the oven is warm or hot, a skilled cook depended more on how hot the oven felt to her hand or on how many seconds it took to brown a bit of flour in a shallow pan. The amount and kind of wood used and the opening and closing of the flue with a damper controlled the blaze. At night in winter every effort was made to bank the fire with coals to keep the fire from dying completely and to keep some warmth in what would, otherwise, be an icy cold kitchen the following morning.

The fire was kindled in one of two ways: by lighting paper and kindling (or turpentine chips or lightnin' pine) or by pouring in lamp oil, or kerosene, and instantly igniting it with the touch of a kitchen match—a large wooden match about 2½ inches long that was stored in a metal container hung near the stove. The later method was tricky, since the flare up from kerosene might singe the hair or cause a burn if the splasher were not careful.

The hottest spots on the surface of the stove are the front eyes; the area at the back is less hot. Thus, moving the pots and pans regulates the amount of heat they are receiving. For example, beans are set to boil at the hottest spot and then moved to the back of the stove to simmer for hours. The quick fire in the front may then be used for making coffee or for other rapid cooking.

In the oven, the hottest spot is, of course, the floor, and it makes the crust of an egg custard pie crisp in a way an electric range cannot. Heat can be regulated while pie-baking by placing the pie on a rack in the middle of the oven or by leaving the oven door open until the inside cools somewhat.

The eyes of the stove could be lifted off, so that the fire could be directly utilized, as when a blaze is needed to singe a chicken and burn off the fine hairs left after it has been plucked.

But perhaps the most constantly appealing attribute of the stove was the coffee pot filled with hot coffee, sitting on a back eye from morning to night as if it were an added appendage. There is even an old saying that when the coffee pot or teakettle rocks from boiling a fresh brew, company's comin'.

Hot water from the teakettle was used to scald a chicken, to wash and rinse dishes, to "hotten up" water in the tin tub used for the proverbial Saturday night bath, and to trickle into cooking beans and other foods.

The mistress of the house was seldom the mistress of the stove (if she could help it); for one of the first things a Southern woman wants, is a cook. "Why, Ah never cooked in mah life," says Miss Lillian. "Ah've always had a cook."

Cooks not only cooked, but they had to do all the food preparation now taken over by the food industry: chickens, for example, had to be killed, scalded, picked, singed, cut up, and salted down. Cooks were proud of their work and to get the noon dinner on, they had to be at the stove early in the morning, so that they wouldn't lose face by serving up a late meal. Cooks also were proud of their territory and whisked a kitchen clean after a meal. Tables and counters were scrubbed; dish towels were washed out and hung up.

The cooks also had to take care of a great deal, if not all, of the washing in a household. For this they used a wash pot, a heavy black iron cauldron that stands on three legs and that doubled for simmering whole hams or making Brunswick or Pine Park, or other stews. The pot might be placed over two of the open eyes of the stove, or, if the weather was hot, over a fire in the backyard. (The night of the Million Dollar Supper in Plains, wash pots were used for making iced tea.)

White garments, sheets, pillowcases, and towels were boiled in the wash pot to cleanse and bleach them. Usually clothes were rubbed over a washboard of ridged tin, the waves of which provided the basis for the expression "washboard road"—a road with deep ruts in it after a heavy rain and one in which cars might easily become mired.

Cooks during the Depression had long hours, and by today's standards, they were overworked and underpaid; yet many worked no harder and had no less cash than their employers. One legendary cook of that era in Plains was Miss Julia Hicks, now 98 and proud of the service she put in. Said her niece, "When Aunt Julia stopped work, her folks gave her a big nice house to live in. That sure does beat Social Security." "Her folks," of course, were her employers.

The tradition continues, and today's Southern cooks can be just as gifted and efficient as their forerunners. By 11:00 a.m. on Wednesday, November 3, 1976, the morning after the late election night, the cook of Mr. and Mrs. Billy Carter had dinner on and order in the kitchen, despite the chaos of the night before.

Plains before 1976 had no restaurants; the cooks did it all. But with the advent of tourism and the Carter boom resulting from the primary and presidential races, the town changed. Mrs. Angie (short for Angieline) Stevens, her two sons, Hampton and Truxdon III, and her daughter Angie Baby opened a restaurant, and the new pastime—for reporters, for visitors, and for some of the townsfolk alike—became sitting in the Front Porch Cafe.

Interior designer Wayne Dean produced a simple, low-budget decor not out of keeping with the rest of Plains. Four old-fashioned revolving fans, like those used in old Southern verandahs, are suspended from the ceiling. There are hanging baskets of green plants. Old shutters painted green cover the top of the short-order kitchen at the back, where a delicatessen is arranged in the manner of a cafeteria. Guests place their orders at the back and take a seat at one of the tables, perhaps in the front corner near an old round ice box on which a green plant has been placed.

The Back Porch Cafe not only provides a culinary oasis of chicken salad and roast beef sandwiches, of homemade pies and potato salad; but it is also a place where people went to "get together"—from Henry Kissinger to a plump Southern lady from Alabama who sat at one of the tables on the Sunday before the November election. She wore a white, crocheted hat with a brim she kept pulling down over her ears; and when she was asked about it, she commented, "Why, I reckon I crocheted it myself. I crochet all the time. . . . I came to Plains to see for myself where he was born. I've been a Democrat all my life, and my father before me never voted anything but a straight Democratic ticket. I tell you, I know Jimmy Carter has been sent to save this country." Reporters and tourists. Advancemen and photographers. Natives and government officials. Trivial talk, important talk, and something happening. The Back Porch Cafe had become the Algonquin of Plains.

V. Vocabulary

Southerners have long been chided by Yankees, carpet-baggers, and other white trash for their manner of speaking. Like the man said who was standing on his head, "It's all relative." Broadcasters use as the norm a steady Midwestern accent (avoid the nasal twang, please), perhaps partly because dictionary pronunciations were concocted in the old days by gnomes of the same background as those who settled the Midwest. The West is fluid; but there is, of course, the Marlboro drawl and other idiosyncrasies.

With the shift of financial and political power to the New South, it may soon be chic to add a few diphthongs here and there, or to adopt the modulated speech with the soothing Southern accent of a Jimmy Carter. New words will come inevitably into the vocabulary as the nation comes to understand the deep South and its traditions.

Some of those words follow in this chapter. But before approaching them, the conscientious Northerner might take a quick look at his own speech patterns and the way in which his words fall on the ears of others. New York is hardly typical ("Shoiman Boining Atlanter"), but is Boston any better? The Atlanta *Constitution* helpfully pointed out that the old mercantile relationships between North and South actually meant that a lot of Northern speech patterns originated in the South. Smug Southerners should therefore apply their usual humility when approaching a brief list of how New Yorkers sound to Southern ears:

BAH: a place to get a drink.
BEEAH: what you sometimes get in a bah.
BOIDS: feathered, winged creatures that sing in trees, if you have any trees.

COIL: a ringlet of hair.

CURL: what snakes do when they get all wrapped up.

DARE: at that spot. As in, "put dat over dare."

DAT: what you just put over dare.

DEEUH: charming, sweet. As in, "Yes, deeuh, I'll be glad to put dat over dare."

FAYUH: equitable. Also, what the cab driver charges.

FEEUH: a feeling one gets when walking alone in New York City parks.

LON GYLAND: where most sane New Yorkers have moved to.

MOIDA: what Brooklynites do to bums.

MUDDER: female parent.

PLEECE: officers of the law. Rarely found in parks.

POCK: a piece of earth in New York City, usually with trees, always with muggers.

TOITY: number that comes after 29.

TRUE: in one side and out the other, as in "he ran true da pock."

WIT: in addition to, or alongside. As in "I'll go wit ya if ya won't go true da pock."[1]

And now, with tongue safely out of cheek, it is only fair to look at some true regional expressions of the South, Georgia style:

A-HOLT: a hold. To get a hold on something. "Hey, man, grab a-holt of that mule."

AILIN': sickly.

ALL DAY SINGING AND DINNER ON THE GROUNDS: a service at the church that includes the church service, dinner spread on tree tables under trees and followed by singing.

AILMINT: an illness or malady.

AIN'T: contraction of am not. "I ain't gonna to do it" means I am not going to do it.

ANTS IN YOUR PANTS: fidgety, a person who cannot sit still.

ARSH PERTATO: Irish potato.

BAD OFF: bad sick or seriously ill.

BAIT: something used to put on a fish hook and also a large quantity of food a person eats. "I'm gonna sit down and eat me a bait of them black-eyed peas," or "I shore had me a bait of catfish."

BAREFOOT AND PREGNANT: an expression men use to describe how they keep their wives.

BOLSTER: a pillow that reaches all the way across the top of a double bed and one used as a base for the usual pillows.

BURNANA: banana.

BURNED OUT: a family that loses its house because of fire is burned out of a home. Before the flames die down and the ashes grow cold, friends and neighbors take the homeless family into their homes and start a campaign to collect clothing, furniture, and money to help the family rebuild.

CENT: instead of saying 10 cents or 50 cents, the custom is to use the singular and say 10 cent and 50 cent.

COMIN' UP A STORM: a storm is brewing. For some reason, people in the South have an inordinate fear of a storm. It may be that lightnin' does strike, though supposedly lightnin' does not strike in the same place twice; and when it does, trees may be struck down and houses set afire. There is a set of unwritten rules that are followed when it is comin' up a storm: Do not sit in front of an open fireplace, window or door. Do not sit with feet on the floor. The best way to be, is to be huddled together in a feather bed.

CORN LIKKER: corn whiskey.

COUNTRY STORE LUNCH: typically, a can of sardines,

crackers, a slice of rat cheese, and a bottle of pop. Men enjoy it, especially men on a construction job. Such a lunch is a treat as compared to a plate of greens, beans or collards, sweet potatoes and corn bread.

CRAP OUT: to squeeze out the tiny sprouts in the top of a plant such as collards.

CUTTIN': a sprig of a flower plant, something else neighbors share. "Miss Virginia, I sho do think you begonia is pretty. Mind if I take a cuttin'?" A cutting placed in water sprouts roots to form the beginning of a new plant.

DARN: a ladylike way of saying damn. Damn is cussin', darn ain't. To darn is a verb meaning to sew with threads in a crisscross manner so as to mend a hole in a sock, sweater, or other garment. Darning was something every thrifty homemaker did after the clothes were washed and ironed and before they were put away. Sometimes, if the darn wore out, a garment was even darned on top of the original darning. A darning egg is a wooden object the size of an egg with a handle. The egg portion was placed in a sock, since darning on the wooden base was easier than without it. If the hole was too big to be darned or if darning were not practical (as in denim overalls), the tear or hole was patched, that is, a piece of matching, or near matching fabric was hand- or machine-stitched or appliqued over the hole. Sometimes patches were placed over worn-out patches. Nothing was thrown away as long as it could be worn.

DOLLS: Miss Lillian said that her two girls, Ruth and Gloria, and a little black girl played together with their dolls. Most dolls were soft, cuddly ones that little girls could mother like babies. Little girls of the 20's and 30's "played house" by drawing off "rooms" on the dirt the way they drew off a hop-scotch frame or the way boys drew off rings for a game of marbles. Such "dollhouses" were quite different from the dollhouse belonging to Mrs. Marylou Whitney, who, with her husband, Cornelius Vanderbilt Whitney, was a guest at the Million Dollar Supper. In 1969 Mrs. Whitney gave her nine-year-old daughter Cornelia a two-ton facsimile of Maple Hill, the Whitney mansion in the bluegrass region of Kentucky.

DOOLUS: lazy; lacking in energy or sense of direction.

DRUNK AS A LORD: smashed on booze.

DRUTHERS: something you prefer to have. "If I had my druthers, I wouldn't go to work today" or "If I had my druthers, I wouldn't clean the house."

ENGAGEMINT: an alliance or engagement between a man and a woman prior to their marriage and also a standing order a peddler fills. Before steady supplies of food in supermarkets, women had regular "engagemints" with farmers or farmers' wives for two pounds butter, two dozen eggs or other quantities every Saturday. The produce was delivered the way a milk man delivered milk to the home. Jimmy Carter as a boy peddled boiled peanuts ("I would earn about $1 per day gross income selling peanuts, and on Saturdays sometimes I could sell as much as five times that amount").[2]

EVER HEAR TELL: have you ever heard. "Did you ever hear tell of anybody doing anything so dumb in your life?"

EVER-WHICHAWAYS: in all directions. "I dropped an egg and hit busted and went ever-whichaways."

EYEBALLIN': talking face to face.

FACE THAT WOULD STOP AN 8-DAY CLOCK: a way of describing an ugly woman.

FALL OUT: fall over in a faint.

FAVORS HIS DADDY: looks like or resembles his father.

FEATHERBED: a comforter filled with feathers. It is used like a quilt. Featherbeds and comforters are warmer than blankets because of the insulation provided by the air spaces between feathers. The thought of getting into bed in a cold, unheated room was abated by the feeling of joy when sinking down into a bed with a bolster and snuggling under a featherbed.

FER: for.

FETCH: get. "Fetch me a pail of water."

FIX: to repair something that is broken; cook a meal, or to rearrange, wash, curl, and comb the hair.

FLESHED UP: a person who has put on weight and a woman who is pregnant.

FINE TOOTH COMB: a flat comb about four inches long and two and one-half inches wide with wide teeth close together on each side. Before electricity and abundant hot water, the custom in lieu of washing was to comb the hair with a fine tooth comb to remove dirt.

FLOW: floor.

FUNERAL FOOD: when there is a death in a home, the first thing the people of Plains do to share the grief and ease the pain, is to start cooking and carrying food to the bereaved home.

During a visit with the Dozier boys, Walter and James, in the office of the Williams' peanut company, one of them commented on rumors about the world outside Plains: "I hear tell that in some cities up North, they have to pay people to be pallbearers for the dead." In Plains, on the other hand, men line up just waiting to be given the privilege.

GEORGIA PEACH: "She is just a Georgia peach" is a complimentary remark about a girl.

GIDDUP: get up and go which is what you say to a horse when you want it to go forward.

GOOBERS: peanuts.

GREEN APPLE QUICK STEP: diarrhea caused by eating apples that are not ripe and other foods.

HARD ROW TO HOE: an expression taken from the fact that packed down garden soil or soil covered with Johnson grass is hard to hoe. Jimmy Carter wrote that when Johnson grass took over a field on their farm, the Carters let the field lay fallow. Any kind of task can be a hard row to hoe.

HAUL OFF: trash and other items are hauled off in a wagon or truck. Haul off is also an expression for winding up the arm and hitting a person. "If you don't shut up, I am going to haul off and hit you."

HEAD OFF: to catch up and stop a person. If a man started to a place along one route, there were usually several alternate routes that could be used—such as riding a horse through the woods—to make a roundabout sweep and come down the road the man was traveling. By approaching him from the opposite direction, the two met head-on and this way the second man could head off the first.

HER'N (HERN): hers.

HIS'N (HISEN): his.

HIT: it.

HIGH AS A GEORGIA PINE: drunk on booze.

HILL OF BEANS: a term used to describe a worthless person or deed. "He ain't worth a hill of beans."

HOPSCOTCH: a children's game in which a child uses a stick to draw a series of blocks on dirt; a chip of wood or little rock is thrown into the squares. The children jump in a pattern and on one foot over the squares. It is a no-cost thing to do and children spend hours playing hopscotch, a good outdoor exercise.

HOT ENOUGH FER YE: in a town where nothing much happens and there is not much to talk about, people talk about the weather; Mark Twain said people talked a lot about it, but nobody did anything. On a hot day, you can be certain of being asked, "Is it hot enough fer ye?"; on a cold day, the expression becomes, "Is it cold enough fer ye?"

HOUND DOG: a hound dog with no special pedigree is part of the population of every Southern town, Plains included. Such a hound dog is not the savvy, sophisticated creature that is part of such hunts as that of the Iroquis Hunt Club in Winchester, Ky., where the fox hunting season begins with the vicar's blessing of the hounds. The Southern hound is more lazy than anything else. When Miss Lillian made a campaign speech in Fayetteville, N.C., where daughter Ruth Carter Stapleton lives, she said of Plains that "a year ago a hound dog could lay down in the street for two weeks and he wouldn't get hit. Now even old ladies have to run." The Elvis Presley recording of "He ain't nothing but a hound dog" expresses a hound's status.

I'LL EAT MY SUNDAY HAT: an exclamation women made (but no one ever did it). A Sunday hat was a woman's prized possession, the way a boy cherished the steelie he used in playing marbles.

IN A FAMILY WAY: pregnant.

IN THE SERVICE: a woman who works as domestic help says of her profession, "I'm in the service." In the service, of course, also means to be a member of the armed forces.

KISSIN' COUSINS: blood is thicker than water, and

those tied by blood stick together. This includes first cousins, and "first cousins onced removed," down to the merest trickle of the same blood. Cousins tend to kiss upon meeting, even if there is no love shared between them. Even if they hate each other, kissin' cousins turn into a united clan in a dispute with others.

LAID BY: crops have to be hoed up to a certain point of maturity when further hoeing is not required. The crops are laid by, an important step that means less work.

LAID UP: sick in bed or confined to the house.

'LASSES: molasses.

LAY DOWN BESIDE WUKK AND GO TO SLEEP: despite the fact there is a lot of work to be done, it is easy to ignore the work and lay down and take a nap or to go to sleep for the night. This practice may partially result from the fact that some people who live in warm climates speak slowly, move slowly, and get sleepier.

LICK AND A PROMISE: when the house needs a thorough cleaning but there is not time to do it along with the other work, a few sweeps or "licks" with the broom and a couple of swings with the dust cloth take care of the most glaring dirt. You put the broom and dust cloth away with a "promise" to clean better the next time.

LIGHT BREAD: the opposite of heavy bread, but it is more than that. The settlers who came from Europe to this country came from a culture where peasants had only dark, heavy bread of the kind now popular with home bakers and natural food enthusiasts. The light white bread was served on the tables of the wealthy. Once bakers in America discovered they could produce the lightest, whitest, fluffiest bread in the world at a price low enough for almost everyone, it became more popular than homemade bread.

Light bread in the south is white bread from the bakery and bread leavened with yeast. It is lighter than breads, such as biscuits, which are leavened with baking powder and/or soda.

LIKE A PIG STY: nothing is messier than the home of pigs; a house that is like a pig sty is plain messy.

LONG SWEETENIN: molasses or syrup that was more abundant than store-bought sugar.

MAKIN' TOGETHER: no relationship to "makin' out," the current expression for what was once called neckin'. Making together is when two or more neighbors team up to prepare something like a batch of peach preserves.

MATER: tomato.

MESS: an untidy room or house. When a person is going in all directions at once and seems to have no set purpose or destination, he may also be a mess. A mess of food is the quantity necessary for dinner at noon, hopefully with enough to "set out" for supper. More than any other time, the word "mess" is used to express fresh vegetables from the garden. "We had our first mess of English peas today" or "Go out and pick a mess of beans." A mess of beans is roughly the quantity a woman can gather up in an ample apron.

MOONSHINE: corn likker or whiskey, so called because it was made illegally in a still, perhaps by moonlight.

MOVING PITCHER OR PICTURE SHOW: the movies are called a moving picture show (just as the school is still the school house and a refrigerator is a "Fridg") because a picture that moves, not to mention one that "talks," is in constrast to nonmoving pictures or photographs.

MR. EARL: calling a man by his first name with Mr. in front of it is an indication not only of respect but of affection. Even though Mr. Earl Carter has been dead for years, the people of Plains speak of him with great respect. The way P. J. Wise pronounces "Mr. Earl," it comes out "Mr. Ul." Mr. Carter as a salutation is more formal and respectful, but not necessarily affectionate.

MYNAZE: mayonnaise or mayo as it is called in delicatessens and sandwich shops. Women, or their cooks, made their own. Little girls also made it. Making mynaze was a Saturday task. A little bowl was held in the lap, eggs were beaten, and oil was added drop by drop. Some cooks used a dinner plate instead of a bowl.

MUSTARD PLASTER: a cloth spread with mustard usually placed on the chest to help sweat out a cold.

NECK OF THE WOODS: a certain part of an area. If two people live in the same part of the country, they live in the same neck of the woods.

NEIGHBORLY: being neighborly is being kind, thoughtful, and helpful. It is reciprocal, and was essential for survival among early settlers. Up until stores offered a steady supply of groceries and daily trips to the store were routine, borrowing a cup of sugar or a couple of eggs was routine between neighbors. A common statement is "that's mighty neighborly of you."

NO FLIES ON HER: a girl or woman with an above-average personality who is turned out as neat as a pin, with no straggly hair, no runs in her stockings, and no smeared make-up.

NOME: contraction of No, Ma'm.

OUTEN FLANNEL: cotton flannel or outing, a favorite fabric for night gowns.

PADDIN' THE STREETS: walking up and down the

streets as something to do. If the area is residential, then it refers to stopping to chat with people, especially in the summer when they are sitting or swinging on the front porch. If in a downtown area, paddin' includes going in and out of stores.

PALLET: a thin quilt placed on the floor as a place for a child to sleep or play. In hot weather, sleeping on a pallet was cooler than sleeping in a bed.

PEACH TREE SWITCH: it was generally conceded that a thin branch cut or broken from a peach tree was the most effective and stinging way to switch the legs of a child.

PEATADS: a little marble made of clay painted in various colors. A handful could be had around 1930 for a nickel.

PEERT: feeling good.

PERTICULAR: Particular or most careful in performing an activity. A Southern lady is "perticular" about how her white damask table cloths are ironed or how a meal is served. Servants know what the lady of the house is "perticular" about and act accordingly.

PITCHFORK: an implement used on the farm for lifting cut hay or pitching it into a wagon. The three-pronged implement the devil is pictured with.

THE PLACE: the home place that included farm, garden, barn, spring house, orchards, bee hives, pig pen, corn crib, chicken house, and privy, or outdoor john. It was a unit almost self-supporting and the basis of the term "we lived off the place."

PLUM WORE OUT: an overworked human body is plum wore out. Shoes and clothing can also be plum wore out.

POKE: a brown paper grocery bag. A poke party is a collection of delectables like sardines, crackers, and cheese bought at the store and spread out as a picnic on torn-open paper bags.

POULTICE: a hot or cold compress placed on the body to treat soreness or injury.

POST OFFICE: the post office on the main street of Plains provides residents not only with a major contact with the outside world but also a place to visit. Postmen in such small offices are able to keep up with the business of people because bills look different from other letters and because letters carry clear postmarks indicating the city from which the letter was mailed.

Post office was also the name of a game boys and girls played at parties. In the game, the boy sent a verbal letter to the girl of his choice. If she answered his letter, he got to kiss her, more often on the cheek than anywhere else.

POUNDIN': the neighborly taking of a collection of foods to a new preacher, a newcomer, or to a family that has suffered a loss such as a fire.

PUT IT ON THE BOOKS: in Plains, where farmers often received payment for their crops only once a year, at the time of the harvest they had little or no cash. When they bought something they said, "Put it on the books," meaning, "Charge it." This was a matter of trust between merchant and customer. Rosalynn Carter used to keep the books and "weigh in" the trucks for the family business. It was a good year for Rosalynn Carter when farmers came to trust a woman to weigh in their trucks. In Plains, the moment of "settling up" was a sacred one, since a farmer got only one payment for his year's crop.[3]

The custom was for the farmer to take the money and pay his creditors. Some were unable to pay in full because of poor yield of crops, sickness in the family, an injury, or other bad luck. Merchants had a choice of carrying the debt "on the books" or acting like a villain in the "Perils of Pauline" movie serial and foreclosing on the mortgage. Through foreclosure, some land barons became owners of more and more property. Some were "land poor," meaning they had considerable land but no cash.

Mr. Earl, Jimmy Carter's father, was a merchant who carried debts "on the books" for years and went to his grave with those debts still being owed him. When Jimmy "made the rounds to the farmers to announce his father's death, they wept. In the last weeks of his life, Earl Carter had canceled some of their loans."[4]

PUTTIN' OUT THE HAND FOR HIM: when a newcomer comes to town, doing something to welcome him. It might be helping him to get a dwelling ready, giving a poundin', taking a meal to the new home, or having a party.

PUTTIN' UP: filling jars with foods and drying to assure supplies for winter.

QUILTIN' PARTY: a quilt is made of small pieces of fabric sewn together, usually by hand, to make covering for a bed. The back of the quilt is plain fabric and a layer of cotton batting is placed between the quilted surface and the back. The various materials are placed on a frame and tacked or quilted with string to hold the three layers in place. Quilting provides an occasion for several women to get together to share a meal or gossip.

RABBIT GUM: a homemade wooden trap somewhat larger than a shoe box. There is an opening at one end topped by a door standing guillotine-like. It drops when triggered by a rabbit entering the trap.

RAISIN': raising. Something a child may or may not

have some of. When a child misbehaves, his mother may scold him with "ain't you got no raisin'?" A "raisin'" is also something done to a log cabin or barn. One man was able to do a lot of the building, but when the time to lift or raise the heavy beams or rafters into place, he needed the help of neighbors who came for a raisin'.

RITE CHEER: right here. "Put the groceries rite cheer."

RITE SMART: the opposite of dumb.

ROSEN EARS: roasting ears, ears of corn that are ready to cook and eat.

RUINT: ruined. "You've done poured paint on your new dress and ruint it.

SEE THE FAVOR: I see the resemblance.

SHORT SWEETENIN': sugar.

SLING SHOT: a weapon made of a forked stick and a rubber band cut from a tire innertube.

SLOP: table wastes collected in a "slop" bucket and used to feed pigs. Also used as a verb: "Go slop the hogs."

SLOW AS MOLASSAS IN JANUARY: a slow person. After molasses or syrup was made in autumn, it was stored in barrels outside in the smokehouse. When the syrup was cold, it ran out very slowly.

SOPPIN': biscuits dipped into a mixture of butter and syrup or sorghum; or dipped into a mixture of red eye gravy and syrup sorghum. There is a real art to soppin', in puttin' the amounts of butter or red eye gravy and syrup or sorghum on the plate so they will come out "even," meaning that everything is finished at the same time, otherwise, you might have to add more butter and/or more sorghum.

The French sop up their luscious sauces with French bread. When they do it, it is sophisticated.

When Southerners do it, it is simply another Southern thing.

SMART AS A PHILADELPHIA LAWYER: as smart as a man could be.

A SPELL: a period of time, as in she sat a spell. A spell also refers to illness: she had a spell, meaning she had the vapors or a case of fainting, or a spell of sickness, especially in the case of an undiagnosed illness.

SPITTIN' IMAGE: a person who looks just like another. "That picture of Jimmy Carter on the big balloon outside the Train Station, it bees the spittin' image of Miss Eleanor Roosevelt."

A SPRING CHICKEN: a young, tender chicken perfect for frying. Before modern breeding methods, there were no broiler-fryers, now available all year long, except in spring when they were called spring chicken. During winter months only mature hens and roosters went on tables. The expression "she is no spring chicken" describes a woman who is no longer young.

STEELIE: a marble of steel about the size of a boy's thumb and larger than the clay marbles, or peatads, placed in the center of a circle drawn in the dirt in the yard. A boy cherished his steelie, which he shot with his thumb into the ring to knock out peatads. The boy, or girl, who knocked out the most peatads won the game.

SWEEPIN' THE YARD: Jimmy Carter wrote that one of his jobs while growing up was sweeping the yard. The lawn around a house was covered with grass that was mowed each Saturday with a small hand-pushed mower which threw out cut grass and filled the air with a special aroma.

Homes also had yards, pure dirt or soil, generally in the area now covered with cement. Chickens roamed the yards where chicken drippings, trash, and leaves collected. Sweeping the trash away with a homemade broom of broom straw or sticks was part of tidying up and Sunday could not come if the yard had not been swept. Po' white trash didn't sweep their yards.

TACKY: an object or deed that is in poor taste. The woman who, in the 30's, dyed her hair a hideous color called hyenna and wore too much make-up and jewelry was tacky. A woman who wears ankle socks with high heel shoes is tacky. A *nouveau riche* woman who orders $400 worth of orchids for a centerpiece is as tacky as her husband if he wears a five-carat diamond ring and two-carat diamond stick pin.

The girl who tries blatantly to take another girl's beau at a dance is tacky, but if she does it subtly and pulls it off; that is fulfilling her role as a Southern belle.

Surrounding oneself with kitsch is tacky, but the most tacky anything or anybody can be is "tacky as homemade sin."

TALL AS A GEORGIA PINE: as tall as anything could be (the Georgia pine was the tallest thing there was before skyscrapers).

TARNATION: a nebulous place somewhere between Heaven and Hell. "Where in tarnation have you been?"

TATER: potato.

THANG: thing.

THAT WAY: pregnant.

TOTE: to carry and now used to describe a bag.

TRECKLY: directly, meaning I will do something when I get to it or when I get good and ready. A child who has been badgering his mother to do something may be told "I'll do it treckly."

TAKIN' IN WASHIN': people picked up dirty laundry at a home and took it to their own home where they washed and ironed and returned the clean laundry to the owner.

TETCHED: touched. "Tetched in the head" means a little loony.

USED TO COULD: there was a time when I could do something. "I used to could run like a rabbit."

WA-AH: war. The Wa-ah most often refers to the War between the States.

WALLER: a hog wallers in mud, meaning it lies down in it.

WUKK: work.

WHITEWASH: an inexpensive, white homemade mixture of lime and water, or of whiting, size and water, used as a kind of paint. Since whitewash is not a sturdy paint, the custom was to whitewash in spring after the rains of winter caused it to wash off. "Too poor to paint, too proud to whitewash."

WHOA: stop; or what you say to a horse when you want it to stop.

YAWL: a term that refers to two or more people, not to one person as people sometimes misuse it who attempt to acquire an instant Southern accent. Start with saying to one person, "Honey chile, how y'awl?"

Y'AWL COME: the invitation to come for a visit is a standing one issued as routinely at the end of a conversation as "How y'awl?" begins a conversation. By all reports, George and Martha Washington kept full house without even issuing an invitation to some visitors who just dropped in. The Washingtons had the comfort of knowing that since two tons of meat had gone into the smokehouse each year, there would be something to put on the table.

VI. Recipes

During the transition to the Carter administration, there appeared a cartoon of a chef wearing an apron with the words "White House Kitchen Transition." Tables were piled high with cartons labeled Butter Beans, Grits, Okra, Hush Puppies, Frozen Barbecue, Snaps, Turnip Greens, Collards. A deliveryman was at the door with a stack of cartons labeled Grits. "Another load of grits, fellas. . . ." he said. "Where's it go? . . . Fellas? . . . Hey! . . ." Another cartoon showed a chef reading a book named "101 Ways to Cook Collards." The implication was that the Carters will be serving a lot of strange, mystical dishes in the White House. Yet the foods are simply the ones they, and other Southerners, grew up on; and there is no mystique about them.

Grits, collards, chitlin's, pigtails, souse meat, liver puddin' and cornbread, all sometimes called soul food, are foods many Southerners have lived on for generations as a way of "holding body 'n soul together."

The people of Plains depend upon their gardens. In an interview in *Family* (October, 1976), Rosalynn Carter says: "We had a cow and a garden." They continue to depend upon foods grown in the garden, but they depend less on their own cows for milk, although folks like

Jimmy Carter remain enthusiasts for dairy products, especially homemade peach ice cream, "rat-trap" cheese, and the Plains' cheese ring.

The following statement made by "Swifty" Lazar, literary agent for former President Richard M. Nixon, in a story about what kind of food Rosalynn Carter will serve in the White House sent out by Women's Wear News Service, brings to mind an old Southern custom called "tarring and feathering," a way of punishing a person by dipping him in hot tar and then coating him with chicken feathers. He said, "American food just isn't suitable for any level of sophistication. If you go American, then you're always favoring some kind of region, and, face it, there's never been a great Southern cook."

Socialite Page Lee Hufty supported the idea of All-American food in the White House. "People who feel we have to serve French food are just insecure," she said. "Americans have fabulous cooks, and various regional foods are interesting; good, Southern food, when it's well done, is some of the most delicious in the world."

Hufty said that baked ham, spoon bread, corn and lobster are state dinner possibilities and that "Americans tend to find security in mimicry, but it takes a certain amount of aplomb to serve American food. Lyndon Johnson had it with his barbecues."

Ogden Nash put it this way:

> "Everybody has the right to think whose food is the most gorgeous, and I nominate Georgia's."

Marshall Fishwick writing about "Southern Cooking" in *The American Heritage Cookbook* said, "Whatever else Southerners may have lacked, they have rarely been short on appetite, or regional delicacies to appease it. Drenched in sunlight, soaked in memory, their land has been well-loved, and their children well-fed."

Guide to Recipes

Chicken and Rice Casserole

One of President Carter's family favorites.

Seasoned pieces of chicken (1 chicken)
½ stick butter
1 4oz. can mushrooms, drained (save liquid)
4 large onions
2 chicken bouillon cubes
1 cup uncooked rice (do not use minute rice)

Melt butter in casserole. Place chicken in layers with onions and mushrooms. Cook covered for 1½ hours at 350 degrees. Remove chicken, add enough boiling water to mushroom liquid to make 4½ cups of broth in casserole. Dissolve chicken bouillon cubes in broth. Add rice; replace chicken and cook covered for one hour.

Chicken and Dumplings

1 5-pound hen, cut into pieces
4 ribs celery
2 slices onion
2 bay leaves
1 ½ teaspoons salt
½ teaspoon pepper
7 cups water
2 cups milk
½ cup flour
Dumplings (recipe below)

Place chicken, celery, onion, bay leaves, salt, pepper, and water in large kettle; bring to a boil, simmer covered for 2 hours or until chicken is tender. Add additional water as needed. Lift out chicken; discard celery, onion, and bay leaves. Skim fat from top of broth; reserve.

Into ⅓ cup reserved fat in kettle, blend flour; add 6 cups broth, heat and stir until smooth. Add milk; taste, add more salt and pepper if needed. Add chicken pieces; heat to a simmer. Add dumplings. Cover and steam for 20 minutes.

DUMPLINGS

2 cups flour, sifted
¼ teaspoon celery salt
4 teaspoons baking powder
¼ teaspoon salt
Pinch of sugar
3 tablespoons chicken fat or butter
¾ cup milk

Sift flour with celery salt, baking powder, salt and sugar. Cut in fat or butter until small even particles are formed. Add milk and blend. Dip a tablespoon first into hot liquid in pot of chicken and then into dumpling batter. Drop the batter by the spoonful on top of the chicken pieces.

Barbecued Chicken

Sprinkle chicken cut into pieces with salt and pepper. Brown in a small amount of fat in a heavy skillet. Cover with barbecue sauce, recipe follows, and cook one hour in a 350 degree oven.

BARBECUE SAUCE

7½ cups tomato juice
1½ teaspoons black pepper
1½ teaspoons red pepper
1½ teaspoons dry mustard
5 teaspoons sugar
5 teaspoons vinegar
½ cup oil
½ cup worcestershire sauce
5 bay leaves
15 cloves garlic, minced
10 teaspoons salt

Mix all ingredients together and bring to a good boil.

Baked Hen

This is a modern workable recipe for the Sunday favorite.

1 4½-to-5-pound roasting chicken
Water
2 bay leaves
A few celery tops
5 or 6 whole peppercorns
½ cup onion, diced
2 to 3 cups celery, diced
¼ cup chicken fat or margarine
½ pound white bread, crumbled
½ 8-ounce package corn bread dressing mix
1¼ teaspoons salt or to taste
¼ teaspoon black pepper
1 tablespoon fresh sage, finely pulverized,
    or 1 teaspoon seasoning

Place chicken in a pot with water to cover. Add bay leaves, celery tops, and peppercorns. Bring water to a boil. Reduce heat to simmer and cover pot. Continue to cook for 1 to 1½ hours or until the chicken is tender but not overcooked. Remove from broth. For dressing, cook diced onion and celery in chicken fat or margarine in skillet until golden. Add to crumbled bread, dressing mix, salt, pepper and sage or poultry seasoning. Add broth to moisten bread mixture. It should be fairly moist (the testing of the recipe took almost 6 cups of broth). Mix and spread into greased shallow baking pan about 10 to 15 inches. Bake dressing in a 325-degree oven for about 45 minutes. Rub the drained chicken with a stick of butter or margarine to hasten browning, and place on top of the dressing. Raise oven temperature to 375 degrees and bake until chicken is hot and brown. Meanwhile, allow broth to boil, uncovered, to reduce in volume. Use broth to make gravy, following the proportion of 2 tablespoons each of fat and flour to each cup of liquid. The fat can be chicken fat. Season with salt and pepper, using a heavy hand with the pepper. Add diced giblets and 3 diced hardcooked eggs. Serve from the gravy boat.

Pecan Stuffing

1 envelope onion soup mix
2 cups boiling water
2 quarts bread cubes
1 cup butter, melted
1½ teaspoons poultry seasoning
½ cup chopped parsley
¾ cup chopped pecans

Combine soup mix and boiling water. Cover and let stand until ready to use. Toast bread. Melt butter, add bread cubes and toss until coated with butter. Mix with remaining ingredients and stuff bird or turn into a greased pan and bake separately in a 375 degree oven until firm.

Fried Chicken

Magnolia Givines stood talking about cooking chicken in the middle of the block of Plains on Wednesday morning, the day it was determined Jimmy Carter was elected President. She said, "I fry every piece of chicken 'til it is exactly the same brown everywhere, no more, no less, no bit of burned." When pressed to explain how she did it, her answer was "I just do it."

Magnolia Givines said she has cooked for 49 years in the home of the late Dr. Benjamin Wise and now cooks for his widow. She also said she is the best cook in town.

To fry chicken, shake pieces of a broiler-fryer in a paper bag that contains flour seasoned with salt and pepper. Shake off excess flour and place in about one-half inch of hot fat—a mixture of oil and shortening—in a skillet. Fry, turning, until each piece "is exactly the same brown."

To make cream or sawmill gravy, pour off fat used for frying chicken, leaving browned portions in pan. For each cup of milk, use a scant 2 tablespoons of the fat drippings and 2 tablespoons flour. Blend flour into drippings, add milk. Cook, stirring, until thickened. Season with salt and pepper.

To make chicken bread, fry biscuit dough cut into biscuits in fat used to fry chicken.

Pressed Chicken Loaf

1 stewing hen, about 4 to 5 pounds
1 tablespoon salt
1 carrot
1 small onion
1 envelope plain gelatin
¼ cup cold water
1 cup finely chopped celery
2 tablespoons chopped canned pimiento
2 tablespoons chopped parsley
1 teaspoon lemon juice
Dash cayenne pepper
4 hard-cooked eggs

Place chicken in large kettle with water to cover. Add salt, whole peeled carrot and onion. Bring to a boil, cover and simmer 2½ to 3 hours or until tender. Let chicken cool in broth in refrigerator overnight. Remove meat from bones and discard bones, fat and skin. Put meat through a coarse meat grinder.

Remove fat congealed on top broth and discard. Heat broth to boiling; strain and broil down to 2 cups. Soften gelatin in the cold water then dissolve it in the hot water. Combine broth with chicken, celery, pimento, parsley, lemon juice, cayenne and finely chopped eggs. Mix well and taste for seasoning. Turn into an oiled loaf pan, 8 by 5 by 3 inches. Chill until firm. Unmold on a platter. Garnish with salad greens, sliced tomatoes, celery curls, radishes or olives. To serve, slice about ½ inch thick. Makes 6 to 8 servings.

Chicken Salad

3 cups cubed cooked chicken
1½ cups diced celery
2 scant teaspoons salt or to taste
¼ teaspoon seasoned salt
¾ teaspoon salt or to taste
½ cup drained salad cubes (diced sweet pickles)
Mayonnaise
Salad greens

Combine chicken, celery, seasoned salt, and salad cubes.
Moisten with mayonnaise; stir to mix. Serve on lettuce.
Makes six servings.

Brunswick Stew

1 large stewing hen, 4½ to 5 lbs.
1 pound lean veal or beef
1 rabbit and/or squirrel, if desired
2 large potatoes, diced
1 large onion diced
4 cups whole kernel corn
4 cups butter beans
2 cans (8 oz. each) tomato sauce
7 teaspoons salt
½ teaspoon pepper
½ teaspoon liquid hot pepper sauce
1 tablespoon worcestershire sauce
⅓ cup butter

Stew chicken, meat, rabbit and squirrel, if used, in water to cover until meat falls from the bones. Cool and shred with the fingers, discarding bones, skin and fat. Put meat back into strained broth and continue to simmer.

In another pot, cook potatoes with onion, corn, beans and tomato sauce in water to cover until potatoes are tender.

Combine vegetables and liquid with meat mixture. The mixture will be thin like soup. Simmer for several minutes until thickened, stirring to prevent sticking. Add seasonings and butter. Makes 4 quarts, more if rabbit and squirrel are added.

Beef Hash

A good way to serve the "Beef Club" meat.

3 tablespoons bacon drippings or shortening
2 cups beef, cooked and diced
3 medium potatoes, boiled and diced
2 onions, diced
1 teaspoon salt
¼ teaspoon pepper
Hot water or beef bouillon

Heat drippings or shortening in skillet; add beef, potatoes, onions, salt and pepper. Cook, stirring occasionally, until mixture begins to brown. Moisten lightly as it cooks with water or bouillon. Serves 6.

Beef Stroganoff

2 pounds round steak
2 cups flour
Salt and pepper
2 large onions, chopped
2 bottles (12 oz. each) chili sauce
½ cup worcestershire sauce
3 cans (10 ½ oz. each) beef bouillon or equal amount
    made from beef bouillon cubes

Cut meat into one-inch cubes; coat in flour seasoned with salt and pepper. Brown meat and onions together in a small amount of fat in a heavy skillet. Add chili sauce, worcestershire sauce and beef bouillon. Cover and simmer one hour or until meat is done. If desired, bake in a 350 degree oven for one hour or until done. Just before serving, stir in sour cream. Makes 8 servings.

—Irene Fletcher

Baked Georgia Country Ham

Scrub thoroughly with a brush. Mold on ham is normal, simply scrub it off before cooking. Place in container large enough to hold it. Add water to cover. Bring to a boil; reduce heat to simmer and begin counting time at that point. Simmer 20 minutes to the pound. Let cool in cool place in cooking liquid if possible. Lift out, slice and serve or, if desired, remove skin, score, glaze as desired and run into a 375 degree oven for 20 minutes or until fat is lightly browned.

To Fry Ham Slices

Cook country ham in just enough grease to keep it from burning in a hot black iron skillet. Cook until fat gets transparent, about one minute. Remove ham from pan.

To make red-eye gravy, add cold water and strong black coffee to skillet, two parts water to one part coffee. Heat and serve.

To cook ham slices in oven, place thin slices in baking pan and put into a cold oven. Turn oven on to 375 degrees. In most ranges the ham is done in 5 to 10 minutes after the oven reaches 375 degrees. Lift ham out of pan. Raise temperature to 450 degrees; put drippings back in to brown and then make into gravy as suggested above.

The oven temperature is right for baking biscuits to serve with ham.

—Angie Stevens

Pig Pickin'

A pig that weighs 70 to 130 pounds dresses down to 50 to 90 pounds. Allow at least one pound per person. A fire of slow-burning wood such as oak or hickory is better for cooking than charcoal that cooks more rapidly.

Cook whole pig, cavity side down, slowly for about three hours for a 60-pound pig and four hours for a 90-pound

pig. Turn carefully and place skin side down. Cook 1 to
1½ hours longer or until done.

Baste throughout cooking with sauce (recipe below).

SAUCE

1 quart water
2 quarts vinegar
2 pounds margarine or butter, optional
¼ pound salt
3 ounces ground hot red pepper or cayenne, or to taste

Combine all ingredients in pot; let simmer for half an
hour before applying to pig. Enough for a 60-pound pig,
dressed weight.

When pig is done, guests step up and pull out the portion of meat and crisp skin they want.

Barbecued Pork

This is the kind of sauce generally used to brush
over fresh pork or chicken as it cooks over charcoal.
The word around Plains is that Thomas Harrell
makes the best barbecue but he "ain't gonna give his
recipe to nobody."

½ cup vinegar
Juice of 1 lemon
2 tablespoons worcestershire sauce
½ teaspoon black pepper
1 teaspoon salt
1 tablespoon sugar
¼ lb. butter, melted.

1 tablespoon prepared mustard
½ cup catsup
Liquid hot pepper sauce to taste

Blend all ingredients together thoroughly. Makes about 1½ cups.

Fried Fatback with Cream Gravy

Place slices of salted fat, salt pork or fatback cut about ¼ inch thick into a cold heavy black iron skillet. Fry slowly over medium heat, turning, until crisp. Remove crisp fat from pan.

Make cream gravy using two tablespoons each of drippings in the pan and flour to each cup of water or milk. Cook, stirring, until thickened. Season liberally with black pepper. It probably has enough salt. Serve with crisply fried white meat. Good served with boiled potatoes.

Ham Hock Dinner

4 ham hocks
Water
4 medium carrots
4 medium onions
4 medium potatoes, halved
½ medium head cabbage, cut into 4 wedges
Salt
Pepper

Cover hocks with water, and simmer for 1½ hours or until meat is tender. Add carrots, onions and potatoes; cook for 15 minutes. Add cabbage with salt and pepper to taste; simmer 10 minutes longer or until cabbage is done. Serves 4.

Souse Meat

The head and feet of a hog make souse meat, a loaf similar to a congealed meat salad. Pork loins, in this recipe developed for today's kitchen, add more meat than the kind prepared on the farm. Souse meat is good served with crackers and beer or other beverages.

5 pigs' feet
4½ pounds pork loin roast, bone-in
1 tablespoon salt
½ teaspoon pepper
5 drops hot pepper sauce
Water
1 cup cider vinegar
3 envelopes unflavored gelatin
⅓ cup cold water
½ cup pimiento, diced and drained

Place pigs' feet and pork roast in large pot; add salt, pepper, and hot pepper sauce with water to cover. Bring water to a boil; reduce heat and simmer for 3 or 4 hours, until the meat is thoroughly cooked. Lift feet and loin from broth. Strain broth and let stand in refrigerator overnight; the next morning remove fat from surface of broth and discard. Meanwhile, pull meat from the bones with the fingers and shred; discard bones and fat but not the skin. Bring skimmed broth to a boil; add vinegar and shredded meat and skin. Taste to determine if additional

Miss Lillian in Plains . . .

. . . taking a break at a Sunday autograph session.

. . . serving cake at a party at The Depot.
PHOTOS CHRISTOPHER FENN

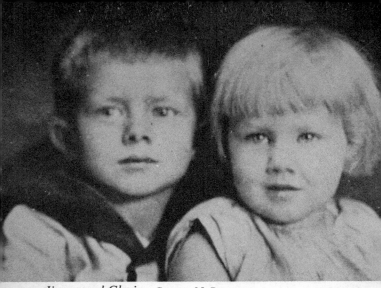

Jimmy and Gloria. CHARLES M. RAFSHOON

Jimmy as a young child.
PHOTOS CHARLES M. RAFSHOON

Jimmy patting his pony.
THE LEDGER-ENQUIRER NEWSPAPERS

Miss Lillian at home.
CHARLES M. RAFSHOON

*James Earl Carter,
father of Jimmy Carter.*
THE LEDGER-ENQUIRER NEWSPAPERS

Jimmy and his dog.
CHARLES M. RAFSHOON

Miss Lillian's father, Jim Jack Gordy.
CHARLES M. RAFSHOON

Jimmy hunting.

*Jimmy and Amy
on the campaign trail.*
PHOTOS CHARLES M. RAFSHOON

*Charles Hicks, proprietor
of The Starlight Club.*

*Sandra Walters in
her store, Sandcraft.*
PHOTOS CHRISTOPHER FENN

Hugh Carter in front of Carter's Antique Store.
CHARLES M. RAFSHOON

Mrs. Allie Smith, Rosalynn Carter's mother.

Downtown Plains. PHOTOS CHRISTOPHER FENN

Jimmy and Martin Luther King, Sr.
THE LEDGER-ENQUIRER NEWSPAPERS

Jimmy visits a classroom, 1970.
CHARLES M. RAFSHOON

Jimmy and Rosalynn, December, 1972.
THE LEDGER-ENQUIRER NEWSPAPERS

Jimmy, Rosalynn and Amy at home.
CHARLES M. RAFSHOON

The Plains Depot and Presidential Campaign Headquarters.

Billy Carter's gas station.
PHOTOS CHRISTOPHER FENN

The Back Porch Café.

Mrs. Fannie Mitchell and Mrs. Edna Ratliff at home.
PHOTOS CHRISTOPHER FENN

*Noted cook
Julia Hicks at home.*

Mrs. Neil Hagerson, Mrs. Milton Hagerson, Tracy Hagerson, and Mrs. L. E. Godwin, III, pouring punch at a campaign party.
THE LEDGER-ENQUIRER NEWSPAPERS

On the campaign trail.
PHOTOS CHARLES M. RAFSHOON

Amy Carter in New York.
CHARLES M. RAFSHOON

Plains High School.
CHRISTOPHER FENN

Jimmy and Billy Carter at Billy's gas station.
THE LEDGER

Plains Hospital, where Jimmy was born.

The Carter's Warehouse.
PHOTOS CHRISTOPHER FENN

Miss Lillian and author Beth Tartan at The Depot.
CHRISTOPHER FENN

Miss Lillian meets the public.
CHARLES M. RAFSHOON

salt and pepper are needed. Simmer slowly for 30 minutes. Soften gelatin in cold water; dissolve in some of hot liquid. Add dissolved gelatin to meat mixture; stir to blend and remove from heat. Add pimiento; pour into loaf pans. Makes 5 loaves, each approximately 9 by 4½ inches.

Salt Pork Milk Gravy

   1 cup salt pork, cubed
   3 tablespoons flour
   2 cups milk
   Salt to taste

In a heavy skillet, cook cubes of pork slowly until crusty and brown or until "crackly and brittle." Remove; drain. Discard all but ¼ cup drippings. Into drippings in pan, blend flour; stir in milk and cook until thickened. Season to taste—little or no salt is needed because of the saltiness of the pork. Add brown cubes; serve over baked or boiled potatoes, or hot biscuits. Makes about 2 cups.

Ham and Sweet Potato Salad

Julia Hicks, who is now approaching her 98th birthday, still cooks regularly for three relatives who live with her in Plains. Her philosophy of life is simple. "Treat your neighbors in the same manner you want to be treated." As for living in Plains, "People here are always willing to help one another out. For example, if you need top-soil you just go over to the Carters (or the Williams) as we did several years ago and ask. Jimmy told us to go down to the warehouse and get what we needed. He never did ask for no money."

On food, "Good Southern Cooking goes hand in hand with Sunday church. My favorite recipes are those which use potatoes in them."

2 cups diced, cooked ham, cut into ½-inch cubes
**2 cups diced, cooked sweet potatoes, cut
      into ½-inch cubes**
1 cup apple, cut in ¼-inch dice
1 cup apple, cut in ¼-inch dice
1 cup fresh orange sections
¼ cup chopped pecans (optional)
1 cup mayonnaise

Gently combine all the ingredients, adding the sweet potatoes last to avoid smashing them. Chill and serve in large lettuce leaves. If you wish, serve with additional mayonnaise.

Serves eight.

Braised Rabbit

1 teaspoon salt
⅛ teaspoon pepper
1 cup flour
1 rabbit, dressed and cut into pieces
1 egg, beaten
1⅓ cups plus 1 tablespoon water
¾ cup dry bread crumbs
4 to 6 tablespoon lard or bacon drippings

Mix salt, pepper, and flour; use to coat pieces of rabbit.

Dip pieces in mixture of egg and 1 tablespoon water, then coat in bread crumbs; brown in hot lard in skillet. Add 1 cup water slowly; cover tightly and simmer 1 hour or until tender, adding remaining water as needed. Makes 6 servings.

Roast Venison

4 to 5-lb venison roast
1 cup wine vinegar
1 cup water
1 large onion, sliced
2 bay leaves
1 whole clove
1 teaspoon dry mustard
1 clove garlic, halved
1 tablespoon salt
1 teaspoon pepper
¾ cup flour
½ cup bacon drippings
3 strips salt pork, ¼ inch thick

Combine vinegar, water, onion, bay leaves, whole clove, mustard, garlic, salt and pepper to make marinade; marinate meat in covered container in refrigerator for 24 hours or longer, turning several times. Lift from marinade; pat dry. Coat in flour; brown on all sides in bacon drippings in heavy skillet. Place in baking pan; place slices of salt pork over meat. Bake in 350 degree oven uncovered for approximately 3 hours or until tender, basting often. Never overcook venison, as it will become dry and lacking in flavor.

Fried Fish

The famous ponds of Plains yield catfish, bream and bass for fried fish and fish-fries.

Sprinkle small fish or fish cut into serving pieces with salt and pepper. Coat in all corn meal or equal parts of corn meal and flour. Fry until crisp and brown in a small amount of fat in skillet, turning to brown on all sides.

Catfish Stew

3 medium-sized potatoes
3 tablespoons bacon drippings
1 large onion, diced
1 pound dressed catfish
3 tablespoons flour
Salt, pepper

Dice peeled potatoes and brown in bacon drippings; add chopped onion and water to cover. Cook slowly for about 20 minutes or until potatoes are tender. Add fish cut into pieces; cook 10 minutes longer or until fish flakes. Thicken with a mixture of flour blended into a small amount of cold water to make a paste. Season with salt and pepper. If desired, fish can also be browned in bacon drippings before adding.

Shrimp Mold

1 large package (8 oz.) cream cheese, softened
1 small package (3 oz.) cream cheese, softened
3 cans (5 to 6 oz. each) shrimp
3 packages (envelopes) plain gelatin
½ cup cold water
½ cup lemon juice
1 cup mayonnaise
1 cup chopped celery
1 medium onion, chopped
1 dash garlic salt
2 dashes liquid hot pepper sauce
1 can (4 oz.) pimiento, drained and diced

Cream cheese until fluffy. Drain shrimp; grind or mince. Blend shrimp into cream cheese. Reserve liquid from shrimp.

Soften gelatin in cold water; add reserved shrimp liquid and lemon juice and heat, stirring, until gelatin is dissolved. Combine shrimp mixture and gelatin mixture; add remaining ingredients. Blend. Pour into a 2-quart mold. Chill until firm. Unmold on salad greens. Garnish as desired. Makes 8 or more servings.

Scalloped Oysters

2 quarts oysters
Salt and pepper to taste
1 quart sweet milk
6 eggs
Crumbled saltine crackers

Heat oysters in milk but do not boil; season with salt and pepper. Beat eggs and add. Place in alternate layers the oyster mixture and cracker crumbs in a baking dish. Pour in milk. Top with crumbs. Bake in a 350 degree oven about 40 minutes or until it bubbles. Dot with butter.

—Irene Fletcher

Butter Beans

There are two ways for cooking fresh butter beans.

1. Cook a slashed chunk of salt pork in water in pot for one hour; add fresh butter beans and simmer one hour or until done in water to cover. The water should cook down gradually. When cooking one quart of beans, the remaining liquid should be about one cup. If water has to be added to keep beans from being too dry, add boiling water a little at a time. For one quart of shelled beans, use ⅛ pound salt pork.

2. Cook beans in salted water to cover slowly for one hour or until done. Water should be reduced as above. Season with butter, ¼ cup per quart of shelled beans, salt and pepper.

Dried Beans

Wash, pick out faulty beans. Soak in cold water overnight or bring beans to a boil in water to cover, remove from heat and soak for an hour. Add to boiling water to cover with a slashed chunk of salt pork, ¼ pound salt pork to one pound dried beans. Some cooks prefer to let the pork simmer for about an hour before adding beans.

Simmer dried beans slowly in a heavy pot two or three

hours adding hot water in small quantities as needed to prevent sticking. Add more salt if needed.

The secret of cooking dried beans to prevent skins from cracking is to do it slowly.

The liquid of cooked pinto beans is the best soup there is in the world, bar none.

The custom is to serve chopped onions covered with vinegar to spoon over cooked dried beans. Green or spring onions are best. There have been thousands of meals in years past that consisted of only a plate of cooked dried beans and hot bread.

Lima Beans

Cook like butter beans. These are a larger and some-what coarser variety and may require longer to cook. Both limas and butter beans are often called butter beans.

English Peas

Best only when peas are young and freshly picked. Cook in salted water to cover for only 15 to 20 minutes. Season with butter, about 1¼ cups butter per quart shelled peas. About a teaspoon of sugar per quart may be added.

Green and Sugar Peas

The same as English peas.

To cook corn with beans or peas, add kernels the last

10 to 15 minutes of cooking time. Corn cooked with butter or lima beans is succotash.

To cook new potatoes with green beans, add scraped, peeled or unpeeled potatoes the last 30 minutes of cooking time. Cook until done.

To cook dumplings with green peas, make dumplings of biscuit dough rolled out like pie crust and then cut into one-inch strips. Place on top of cooked peas with an additional pat of butter. Be sure there is sufficient cooking liquid to prevent burning. Cover and steam 10 to 12 minutes.

To prepare green peas and new potatoes, cook new potatoes separately. Combine with cooked green peas and add a medium thick cream sauce. Frozen green peas, especially the tiny little ones, are an excellent substitute for fresh peas.

Cooking Collards

Cook with salt pork, but only until tender. Cook the bud leaves, the tender inner leaves, about 10 minutes, cook the outer or more mature leaves for 15 to 20 minutes. If prepared in a pressure cooker, turn it off as soon as the pressure is up.

One cook insists collards do not reach their full flavor potential unless seasoned with a bit of possum grease.

Here is another way.

Cook a piece of old ham until partly done in water to cover; add collards that have been washed and ribs removed. Cook collards until done; lift out of the cooking liquid. Chop greens finely and add salt to taste if needed. Spoon some of the cooking liquid over the greens.

Collards and Corn Meal or Pot Dumplings

In a large pot cook a gashed chunk of salt pork that weighs ⅓ to ½ pound in water to cover for 10 minutes.

Remove coarse ribs from three pounds of collard greens; cut into strips and add to pot. Bring to a boil; reduce heat to medium and cook until collards are tender, 20 to 30 minutes or more. Drain off most of the liquid; reserve liquid.

Fry three or four slices of bacon; pour drippings over collards and cut through them with a knife.

Add sufficient of the reserved liquid to plain corn meal with a little salt to make a mixture that can be shaped to make a pone or dumpling like a small hamburger patty. Place patties on top collards and cook like dumplings.

Fried Collards

After a frost, select two plump bunches of collards. Look, wash and remove coarse stalk; cut out large stems.

Roll two or three leaves in a roll and cut into shreds; repeat until finished all leaves. Place shreds in cold water in a mixing bowl; let stand 20 minutes or longer. The shreds will become quite brittle.

In a skillet, fry out some slices of fatback or salt pork; add some corn oil to drippings. Add drained shredded collards to grease; cover and simmer for 30 to 40 minutes, stirring. Add salt to taste. Delicious with cracklin' corn bread.

Another way is to boil collards with salt pork; drain.

Chop an onion or two; fry in drippings. Add drained collards; heat.

Some cooks like to add a pod or two of red pepper to water used for cooking collards.

Fresh Greens and Potatoes

>   ½ pound fresh turnip greens
>   ½ pound fresh kale
>   ½ pound fresh spinach
>   2 tablespoons bacon drippings
>   2 cups diced uncooked potatoes
>   ¼ cup boiling water
>   1½ teaspoons salt, or to taste
>   ½ teaspoon sugar
>   ¼ teaspoon pepper
>   Dash cayenne
>   6 strips crisp cooked bacon
>   Herbed bread crumbs sauce, recipe follows

Wash greens thoroughly. Place bacon drippings in a 3-quart saucepan. Add turnip greens, kale, potatoes, water, salt and sugar. Cover and cook 15 minutes. Add spinach and cook 5 minutes or until spinach is wilted. Add pepper. Toss lightly, being careful not to mash the potatoes. Serve with bacon strips and this crumb sauce.

HERBED BREAD CRUMB SAUCE

Melt ¼ cup butter or margarine in a saucepan. Add ⅛ teaspoon marjoram and 1 cup of bread crumbs. Stir and cook until butter has browned lightly. Makes 4 to 6 servings.

Grits 'n Greens

GRITS:

1 cup white hominy grits
5 cups boiling water*
1 teaspoon salt

TURNIP GREENS:

1 lb. hog jowl or ham hock
4 cups water
1 teaspoon salt
3 lb. turnip greens washed and drained

For grits, slowly stir into boiling salted water. Cover and cook slowly 25 to 30 minutes, stirring frequently. Serve with gravy or butter and turnip greens (see below).

For greens, simmer meat in water about 45 minutes. Add salt and turnip greens; cook until tender. Drain. Makes 6 servings.

*NOTE: To use quick grits, decrease water to 4 cups. Cook uncovered 2½ to 5 minutes, stirring occasionally.

Cheese Grits Casserole

A favorite of Sybil Carter (Mrs. Billy) who one interview said Miss Lillian thinks "is the greatest since egg cartons."

    1 cup quick-cooking grits
    3 cups boiling water
    1 teaspoon salt
    ½ cup (1 stick) margarine
    1 roll (6 oz.) garlic cheese
    2 eggs
    Milk
    Coarse cracker crumbs
    Paprika

By package directions, cook grits in boiling water. Meanwhile, melt together margarine and cheese; add to hot cooked grits. Beat eggs and turn into measuring cup; fill cup with milk. Stir egg mixture into grits and cheese. Pour into a buttered casserole. Top with cracker crumbs; sprinkle with paprika. Bake in a 350 degree oven for 40 minutes or until firm. Serves 6.

Fried Okra

Place whole fresh okra pods in a colander; wash under running water. While okra is still moist, cut into one-inch lengths. Shake in flour seasoned with salt and pepper in a brown bag, the same one used for coating pieces of chicken for frying.

Lift coated okra pieces out of flour with hands, or

slotted spoon, onto a plate. At this point, there is an excess of flour on the okra. Lift and shake pieces with hands or slotted spoon and place on another plate.

Have about ¼ inch of oil heating in a heavy skillet. The oil should be hot, but not smoking. Lift okra from plate, and continue to shake off excess coating. Place okra in hot fat; cook quickly, stirring, until coating is brown and crisp. Lift out browned pieces with slotted spoon. Serve immediately.

Okra is tender and requires little or no cooking beyond the browning. If oil is too hot or okra is cooked too long, it will be burned.

Gumbo Vegetables

    1 large onion, diced
    ¼ cup diced green pepper
    2 tablespoons salad oil
    1 8-oz. can tomato sauce
    1 can (no. 2½) tomatoes
    3 medium potatoes, diced
    1 bay leaf
    ¼ teaspoon thyme
    1 teaspoon worcestershire sauce
    1 10-oz. package frozen okra
    1 10-oz. package frozen corn

Sauté onion and pepper in oil until soft. Add tomato sauce, tomatoes, potatoes and seasonings. Cover and cook gently about 15 minutes. Add okra and corn and continue cooking until done. Makes 8 or more servings.

Rice Casserole

½ stick butter or margarine
1 can (10½ oz.) onion soup
1 can (10½ oz.) chicken broth
1 chicken bouillon cube or teaspoon chicken
    bouillon dissolved in broth
1 cup uncooked rice
1 can (4 oz.) mushroom stems and pieces
¼ cup slivered almonds

Melt butter; add drained mushrooms, almonds and rice and cook several minutes. Add soup, broth and dissolved bouillon. Turn into a 1½ quart casserole. Bake, covered, for 1 hour at 350 degrees. Uncover and stir carefully.
—*Betty Carter (Mrs. Alton Carter)*

Baked Tomatoes

12 firm ripe tomatoes
1 pound bacon
1 medium onion, chopped
4 teaspoons Lea and Perrins sauce
2 teaspoons hot pepper sauce
1 cup chopped celery
1 cup saltine crumbs
Pepper to taste

Wash tomatoes; core out insides and reserve portion removed. Cook bacon in a skillet until crispy; drain.

In a small pan, combine chopped insides of tomatoes,

celery and onion and cook until tender, about five minutes. Add seasonings and simmer five minutes. Remove from heat; add crumbled bacon and crumbs, and a bit of bacon drippings for flavor; stuff into tomatoes. Dribble melted butter over the top. Bake for 15 minutes in a 350 degree oven.

—Irene Fletcher

Scalloped Tomatoes

1½ cups stale bread, in coarse pieces
¼ cup butter, melted
2 cups canned tomatoes
1 teaspoon salt
6 tablespoons brown sugar

Place bread in 9-inch baking dish 2 inches deep; pour butter over bread, and stir to coat pieces. Meanwhile, in saucepan heat tomatoes, salt and sugar to boiling point; pour over bread. Bake in a 425-degree oven for 25 minutes or until well browned. Serves 6.

Asparagus Casserole

3 cans (No. 2) green asparagus tips
6 hard cooked eggs
2 sticks (1 cup) butter
1 cup flour
1 quart (4 cups) milk
Salt, pepper
½ pound Cheddar cheese, grated

Drain asparagus. Slice peeled eggs.

Make a thick cream sauce of butter, flour and milk; season to taste with salt and pepper.

In a baking dish arrange asparagus and egg slices in layers. Pour sauce over the top; sprinkle with cheese. Bake in a 350 degree oven for 30 minutes or until bubbly. Serves 20.

—*Irene Fletcher*

Corn Pudding

½ pound bacon
1 can (16 ounces) creamstyle corn
1 can (12 ounces) whole kernel corn, drained
2 eggs, beaten
¼ cup minced onion
2 tablespoons chopped parsley
¼ teaspoon salt
¼ teaspoon pepper

Cook bacon until almost crisp; drain. Crumble and combine with remaining ingredients. Pour into greased casserole. Bake in a 375 degree oven for 20 minutes or until bubbly. Makes 6 servings. If desired, sprinkle with buttered bread crumbs before baking.

Grated Yam Pudding
(Sweet Potato Pudding)

4 cups grated raw sweet potatoes, packed
Salted ice water
1¾ cups granulated sugar

1 cup undiluted evaporated milk
½ cup whole milk
Cinnamon
1 stick margarine
Marshmallows

Soak potatoes in salted ice water to cover for 15 minutes. Drain thoroughly and combine with sugar, milks and turn into baking pan. Sprinkle with cinnamon; dot with butter. Bake in a 350 degree oven for a little over 1 hour or until done. Remove from oven; top with marshmallows and run back in oven to melt marshmallows.

Sweet Potato Casserole With Crunchy Topping

3 cups mashed sweet potatoes (1 no. 2½ can may be used)
1 cup sugar
½ teaspoon salt
⅓ stick margarine melted or soft
½ cup evaporated milk
1 teaspoon butter flavoring
1 teaspoon sherry flavoring
2 eggs, beaten
Topping (see below)

Combine potatoes, sugar, salt, margarine, milk, flavorings and eggs; turn into greased baking dish.

CRUNCHY TOPPING

Sprinkle with topping made by blending 1 cup brown sugar, ⅓ cup flour, ⅓ stick margarine and 1 cup chopped nuts. Bake in a 350 degree oven for 35 minutes.

Tropical Sweet Potato Casserole

Hostesses have made considerable use of this dish.

4 cups mashed cooked sweet potatoes
1 cup drained, crushed pineapple
4 tablespoons melted butter or margarine
1 teaspoon salt
¼ cup brown sugar
⅛ teaspoon cinnamon
½ cup coconut

Combine mashed sweet potatoes with ¾ cup of the pineapple, 3 tablespoons of the butter or margarine, salt, brown sugar and cinnamon. Beat well. Heap in a 1½ quart casserole. To rest of melted butter, add coconut and remaining pineapple, mix well and sprinkle over top. Bake at 375 degrees about 40 minutes. Makes 6 servings.

Sweet Potato Pone

2 large or 3 medium sweet potatoes
Grated rind of lemon and orange
2 eggs beaten
½ cup brown sugar
½ teaspoon cinnamon
½ teaspoon nutmeg
½ teaspoon ground cloves
½ cup molasses
1 cup milk
½ cup (1 stick) margarine, melted

Peel sweet potatoes and shred on the shredding side of the grater. Add lemon and orange rind. Beat eggs and sugar and stir into potato mixture with spices, molasses, milk and melted margarine.

Turn into a buttered baking dish. Bake in a 350-degree oven for 1 hour or until done. Serve hot. Makes 8 or more (most likely more) servings.

Orange Glazed Sweet Potatoes

6 medium-sized sweet potatoes
½ cup dark brown sugar, firmly packed
½ cup granulated sugar
1 tablespoon cornstarch
½ teaspoon salt
½ cup frozen orange juice concentrate
¼ cup margarine

Boil sweet potatoes in their jackets about 20 minutes or until almost tender. Cool, peel, cut in thick slices. Place in greased shallow baking dish.

Combine sugars, cornstarch and salt in saucepan. Add orange juice concentrate and cook, stirring constantly, five minutes. Add margarine and when it is melted, pour over potatoes. Bake in a 375 degree oven for 25 to 30 minutes. Make 6 servings.

Peanutty Supreme Squash

>   2 **pounds yellow crookneck squash**
>   2 **ounces pimiento, drained and diced**
>   2 **tablespoons grated onion**
>   2 **carrots, grated**
>   1 **can (10½ oz.) cream of chicken soup**
>   1 **cup sour cream**
>   1 **package (7 ounce) herb stuffing mix**
>   1 **stick margarine, melted**
>   1 **cup chopped salted peanuts**
>   **Salt if needed**

Slice squash and cook in a small amount of water until tender; drain and mash. Add pimiento, onion, carrots, soup and sour cream and blend. Toss together stuffing mix, margarine and peanuts; turn half into a casserole. Pour in squash mixture; top with remaining crumb mixture. Bake in a 375 degree oven for 30 minutes or until bubbly. Serves 8 to 10.

Butternut Squash Souffle

This is a favorite recipe of Rosalynn Carter.

2 cups cooked butternut squash, mashed
1 cup milk
½ to 1 stick margarine
1 cup sugar
3 eggs, whole
Flavoring as desired (1 teaspoon ginger is good
      —some cinnamon)

Mix all ingredients and put in baking dish. Cook at 350 degrees for 40 minutes. Stir once during baking.

Calico Squash

2 cups cooked, drained summer squash
1½ cup medium white sauce
¼ pound grated sharp Cheddar cheese
¼ cup chopped pecans
¼ cup chopped pimiento
Crushed potato chips

Mix all ingredients except potato chips and pour into casserole. Top with crushed potato chips. Bake in a 350 degree oven for 20 minutes. Makes 6 servings.

Squash Casserole

2 cups cooked mashed squash
1 cup bread crumbs
1 cup milk
4 tablespoons bacon drippings
2 eggs, beaten
1 onion, grated
Salt and pepper
1 to 1½ cups grated sharp cheese
½ teaspoon baking powder
½ roll of crushed Ritz crackers
¼ to ½ stick margarine, melted

Scald milk; add bacon drippings; pour over bread crumbs, then combine with squash. Add eggs, onion, salt and pepper to taste, cheese and baking powder. Turn into buttered casserole. Top with cracker crumbs and melted margarine. Bake at 350 degrees for 30 minutes. Virginia Carter: "When the John Glenns came to Plains to visit the Carters, I fixed dinner for them and Annie Glenn loved this casserole and asked me for the recipe."

Potato Salad

7 or 8 medium-sized potatoes
4 hard cooked eggs
6 ribs celery
3 large dill pickles
2 medium-sized bell peppers
1 large onion

¼ cup prepared mustard
¼ cup vinegar
2 tablespoons salad oil
1 teaspoon salt
¼ teaspoon pepper
¾ cup mayonnaise, approximate

Cook unpeeled potatoes in water to cover until tender but not soft; drain. Pry open with forks to allow steam to escape. Place pot back on warm burner turned off, to allow potatoes to dry. When cool, peel and dice potatoes.

Dice eggs, celery, pickles, and peppers and onions; add to potatoes. Combine mustard, vinegar, oil, salt and pepper; stir into potato mixture. Add sufficient mayonnaise to moisten. Makes 10 or more servings.

Superb Green Salad

2 No. 303 cans French-style green beans
1 No. 303 can green peas
¼ cup stuffed olives, sliced
1 cup celery, sliced
1 cup carrots, sliced
1 cup green onions with some tops, sliced
1 cup frozen large green lima beans, cooked, optional
¼ cup salad oil
¼ cup vinegar
½ teaspoon worcestershire sauce
½ teaspoon paprika
⅔ cup powdered sugar or to taste
1 teaspoon salt

Drain all vegetables and combine. Mix remaining ingredients and pour over vegetables. Cover and chill for 4 hours. It will keep for several days. Makes 16 to 18 servings.

Springtime Salad

2 quarts leaf lettuce, shredded
4 radishes
1 large dill pickle, diced
2 tomatoes, diced
4 slices bacon, fried crisp
1 cup hot red eye gravy

Place lettuce in a large platter or bowl; top with radishes, onions, pickles, tomatoes, and bacon. Just before serving, pour on hot red eye gravy. Makes 6 servings.

Refrigerator Coleslaw

1½ pound head cabbage
1 medium onion, finely chopped
½ green pepper, finely chopped
¼ cup plus one tablespoon sugar
½ cup salad oil
½ cup vinegar
½ teaspoon dry mustard
1 teaspoon salt
½ teaspoon celery seed

Chop or shred cabbage and place it in a bowl with onion and green pepper. Sprinkle with ¼ cup sugar and toss lightly to blend.

In a saucepan, combine remaining sugar and other

ingredients; bring to a boil. Pour, while hot, over the cabbage mixture. Toss to mix. Chill, covered, for at least 4 hours. It will keep for days in the refrigerator. Makes about 2 quarts.

Mayonnaise

1 whole egg or 2 egg yolks
½ teaspoon dry mustard
1 teaspoon salt
2 tablespoons vinegar
1 cup salad oil

Into the container of the electric blender, put the egg or egg yolks, mustard, salt, vinegar, and ¼ cup salad oil; cover container and flick motor on and off high speed. Remove cover, turn motor on high; immediately add remaining oil in a steady stream. When all the oil is added, turn off motor. Makes 1¼ cups.

Pineapple Dill Pickle Salad

Fantastic flavor, excellent with baked ham.

2 cups sugar
1½ cups water
1 whole box (3 one-oz. envelopes) plain gelatin
1 cup water
1 cup orange juice
5 large dill pickles
1 can (20 oz.) crushed pineapple

In a saucepan, combine sugar and 1½ cups water; boil for 10 minutes.

Soften gelatin in one cup cold water; heat, stirring gently until gelatin is dissolved. Remove from heat; add orange juice.

Grind pickles; drain off juice and reserve. Drain pineapple; reserve juice. Add ground pickles to crushed pineapple. Add a mixture of 2 cups reserved pickle juice and liquid drained from pineapple—that is a total of 2 cups in all not two cups of each pickle juice and pineapple juice.

Mix together sugar-water mixture, gelatin-orange juice mixture and pickle-pineapple mixture. Turn into a mold and chill until firm. Serves 10.

—*Angie Stevens*

Jellied Grapefruit Pecan Salad

2 No. 2 cans grapefruit sections
1 envelope plain gelatin
¼ cup sugar
½ cup chopped celery
½ cup chopped pecans

Drain juice from grapefruit. Soften gelatin in ½ cup juice. Heat 1½ cups juice to boiling and use to dissolve gelatin. Add sugar and cool. Add remaining ingredients and pour into molds. Chill until firm. Serve on crisp salad greens. Makes 6 servings.

Fried Apples

An ideal apple for frying is a green apple called the June apple, which ripens in early summer. The Rambo, which ripens in midsummer, and the Stayman Winesap are also good. The June apple and the Rambo tend to become mushy when cooked.

6 medium or 8 small tart apples
⅓ cup bacon drippings or mixture of salad oil and margarine
½ to ¾ cup sugar

To prepare, core unpeeled apples and cut into slices ¼ inch thick. Heat drippings or oil and margarine in heavy skillet; add apple rings. Cook over moderate heat, lifting apple slices as they brown lightly to the top. Continue to cook, until all the apple slices are almost soft. If needed to prevent sticking, add more drippings or margarine and oil. Sprinkle with sugar, reduce heat to low and cook for about 15 minutes more or until done. Makes 6 servings.

Okra Pickle

3½ pounds small okra pods
1 pint distilled vinegar, white
1 quart water
⅓ cup salt
3 small hot peppers, if desired
Garlic cloves
2 teaspoons dill seed

Pack okra firmly in hot sterilized jars. Put a garlic clove in each jar. Pour boiling brine in jars and seal. Process in boiling-water bath at simmering temperature—about 180-200 degrees—for 10 minutes. Let ripen several weeks before opening. Yield: 4 to 5 pints.

Pickled Peaches

Clingstones are best for pickling, but freestone peaches may be used.

1 piece ginger root
2 sticks cinnamon
1 tablespoon whole allspice
1 tablespoon whole cloves
2 cups sugar
2 cups water
3 cups vinegar
24 small firm-ripe, peeled peaches
2 cups sugar
1 to 2 cups sugar

Tie spices in a cheesecloth bag. Add spice bag, 2 cups sugar and water to vinegar. Bring to boiling, add peaches, a few at a time; simmer until heated thoroughly. Carefully remove peaches. Repeat until all peaches have been heated. Pour boiling syrup over peaches; cover and let stand 3 to 4 hours. Carefully remove peaches from syrup. Add 2 cups sugar to the syrup and heat to boiling. Pour over peaches; cover and let stand 12 to 18 hours in a cool place. Pack peaches into hot jars, leaving ¼-inch head space. Add remaining 1 to 2 cups sugar to syrup. Bring to boiling, pour over peaches, leaving ¼-inch head space.

Adjust caps. Process pints and quarts 15 minutes in boiling-water bath. Yield: about 6 pints.

Watermelon Rind Pickles

Prepare rind (approximately 6 lbs.) from 1 watermelon
¼ cup salt
3 tablespoons powdered alum
4 cups cider vinegar
3 cups water
8 cups sugar
5 sticks cinnamon
1½ tablespoons whole cloves

Prepare rind by peeling away green skin. Leave a little of the pink portion, if desired, for a touch of pink makes a prettier pickle. Cut into squares or fancy shapes as desired.

Dissolve salt in 1 gallon cold water and pour over prepared rind. Let stand for three hours. Drain and rinse in cold water. Stir alum into 2 gallons water and add to rind. Bring to a boil, reduce heat and simmer 30 minutes. Drain and rinse. Add another gallon of water and simmer until tender but not soft, 30 to 45 minutes.

Heat vinegar, 3 cups water and sugar to a boil. Tie spices in a bag and add with rind. Cook slowly, uncovered, until syrup is thickened, about one hour. Pack hot into hot sterilized jars. Seal.

Red Pepper Relish

Excellent sweet-sour with meat.

7 cups finely chopped sweet red peppers (14 to 16 medium)
2 tablespoons salt
6 cups sugar
1 quart vinegar

Combine peppers and salt; let stand 3 to 4 hours. Add sugar and vinegar; cook, stirring frequently, until thick, about 45 minutes. Pour, boiling hot, into hot jars, leaving ⅛-inch head space. Adjust caps. Process 10 minutes. Yield: about 6 half-pints.

Hot Bread

Serving hot bread hot is a way a cook pampers her family and compliments her guests (because it is quick to make, it also solves the problem of baking bread in hot weather). The hot breads cooks brought to the Million Dollar Supper were baked at the last moment and brought while still warm.

At the recent family reunion a guest reports that a chart was posted in the kitchen giving the exact times pans of cornbread went into the oven, and the names of men were also posted so that two pans of hot cornbread went to the table at a time.

Hushpuppies

Maxine Reese says Norman Murray makes the best hushpuppies.

1¾ cup cornmeal
1 teaspoon salt
4 tablespoons flour
1 teaspoon baking powder
6 tablespoons chopped onion
1¾ cup boiling water

Mix and sift all dry ingredients. Add chopped onion and beaten egg. Pour boiling water over this mixture, stirring constantly until mixture is smooth. Drop by spoonfuls into deep hot fat. Makes about 6 servings.

Fried Corn Cakes

These are a speciality of the Americus Country Club run by Irene Fletcher and her husband, Leonard, for 27 years.

2 cups plain corn meal
1 teaspoon salt
1 cup canned undiluted evaporated milk
3 tablespoons oil

Blend together corn meal, salt and milk until smooth. Batter must be thin. If not thin enough, add water to make the right consistency.

Heat oil in a heavy black iron skillet until a drop of water dropped into it "sputters." Spoon batter by the spoonful into the hot oil that should not be too hot. Turn lacy cakes several times until real crisp.

All Corn Muffins

1 cup corn meal
1 teaspoon salt
1 cup boiling water
½ cup milk
1 egg
2 teaspoons baking powder
1 tablespoon melted butter

Mix corn meal and salt. Add boiling water. Stir and then add milk. Stir well. Add egg and blend.

Just before pouring into greased muffin tins, stir in baking powder and melted butter. Bake at 475 degrees for 12 minutes or until well browned. Serve at once.

Angie Stevens' Crackling Corn Bread

2 cups cornmeal
2 cups cracklings
1 teaspoon salt
1 teaspoon baking powder
Water
Butter

Combine cornmeal, cracklings, salt and baking powder; add sufficient water to make mixture of a consistency that can be shaped with the hands into little pones. Bake in a greased baking pan in a 350 degree oven until brown. "Butter the tops the minute they are brown."

Hominy Spoon Bread Casserole

1 No. 2 can whole hominy
2 eggs
1½ cups milk
½ cup corn meal
2 tablespoons melted butter
1 teaspoon salt

Drain hominy well. Beat eggs and add milk, corn meal, melted butter and salt. Blend well together and add hominy.

Pour into buttered shallow pyrex baking dish. Bake at 300 degrees for 45 minutes or until firm. Makes 6 servings.

Angel Biscuits

5 cups flour
¼ cup sugar
3 teaspoons baking powder
1 teaspoon baking soda
1 teaspoon salt
1 cup shortening
1 package dry yeast
2 tablespoons warm water
2 cups buttermilk
¼ cup butter or margarine, melted

Sift together flour, sugar, baking powder, baking soda, and salt. Stir in shortening. Meanwhile, dissolve yeast in warm water. Add with buttermilk to flour mixture. Mix well. If necessary, add additional flour to make soft dough. Turn out on lightly floured board. Roll out to ¼-inch thickness. Cut with round biscuit cutter. Brush with melted butter and fold over to make pocketbook rolls. Bake in a 400-degree oven for 15 minutes or until lightly browned. The dough does not have to rise before baking. The dough may be stored in the refrigerator before baking.

Yeast Rolls

2 packages dry granular yeast
2 cups warm water
¾ cup sugar
¾ cup shortening
1 cup mashed potatoes
2 eggs
1 tablespoon salt
Flour

Dissolve yeast in warm water and let stand until well dissolved. Add sugar, shortening, potatoes (they should be mashed quite fine), eggs and salt and mix "real good."

Add flour to make a fairly stiff dough. Knead well. Cover and let rise in a warm place until almost doubled in bulk. Work down and let rise again until almost double in bulk.

Work out into "small biscuits" and place side by side but not too close together in a greased baking pan. Let rise until almost double in bulk. With a pastry brush,

brush with melted butter. Bake in a 350-degree oven until done. The time it takes is "just accordin'."

Tea Rolls

2 packages dry yeast
½ cup water, lukewarm
¼ cup sugar
½ cup milk, scalded
1 teaspoon salt
½ cup plus 2 tablespoons butter, melted
3 eggs, beaten
4½ cups flour, sifted, approximate

Stir yeast into water, let stand for a few minutes, then add sugar. Pour hot milk over salt and ½ cup butter; let stand until lukewarm, add yeast, eggs, and flour to make a soft dough. Turn out on floured board; knead lightly. Place in bowl, cover; let rise in a warm place until double in bulk; punch down. Roll out dough on floured board to ¼-inch thickness; cut with 2-inch-round cutter. Fold each piece in half with top slightly overlapping bottom. Place on baking sheet, and brush with remaining melted butter; let rise in warm place until almost double in bulk. Bake in a 425-degree oven for 15 minutes or until done. Makes about 4 dozen.

Buttermilk Rolls

1 **packaged dry granular yeast**
2 **cups buttermilk**
5 **cups sifted flour**
3 **tablespoons sugar**
1 **teaspoon salt**
¼ **teaspoon baking powder**
¼ **teaspoon soda**
4 **tablespoons shortening**

Heat about ½ cup of the buttermilk to lukewarm. Sprinkle the package of yeast over the lukewarm milk and stir until dissolved. Allow to stand a few minutes and then add remaining buttermilk. Blend well.

Sift flour with dry ingredients and work in shortening as for biscuits. Add buttermilk mixture and blend well. Grease the top of the dough. Cover and store in the refrigerator.

About two hours before serving time, turn the dough out on a lightly floured board and knead gently. Make into rolls and place on greased baking sheet. Brush tops with melted butter.

Allow to stand in a warm place until about double in bulk. Bake at 400 degrees for 12 to 15 minutes or until done.

The dough will keep beautifully in the refrigerator for several days.

Superb Yeast Bread

2½ cups quite warm (almost hot) water
3 tablespoons sugar
1 tablespoon salt
¼ cup shortening
2 packages dry yeast
6½ cups sifted flour
¾ cup dry milk powder

Measure warm water into a saucepan or bowl with cover. Add sugar, salt, shortening and yeast and stir together. Cover tightly. Measure flour and milk powder into large bowl. Add yeast mixture and stir until well blended. Turn out on lightly floured board and knead until ingredients are well blended and mixture is smooth and springy (usually no more than 3 minutes).

Place in warmed bowl which has been liberally greased, turn dough over to get grease on top of dough, cover with damp towel and place in oven. Turn oven on to "preheat" for 30 seconds only. Turn off heat.

Let rise 45 minutes—dough will be up to top of bowl—punch down, turn over, return to oven.

Let rise again for 15 minutes. Dough will not be quite to top of bowl. Turn out on floured board and divide into two parts. Cover dough with towel and let rest while greasing two loaf pans. Shape dough into two loaves and place in pans.

Return loaves to oven, warming it a little if heat has been lost. Let stay in oven for 15 to 20 minutes—the dough will have doubled in bulk but will not fill pan.

Turn on oven to 400 degrees. From the time the oven is turned on to 400 degrees, bake 35 minutes.

Cream Cheese Pound Cake

Everybody in Plains talks about this cake that Marle Leah Carter, the thirteen-year-old daughter of Sybil and Billy Carter, bakes.

3 sticks (¾ lb.) butter
1 package (8 oz.) cream cheese, softened
3 cups sugar
6 eggs
1 teaspoon vanilla flavoring
1 teaspoon almond flavoring
3 cups flour

Cream together butter and cream cheese, blending in sugar. Add eggs, one at a time, and continue to blend. Add flavorings and flour; blend until smooth. Do not overbeat.

Pour batter into a greased and floured tube pan. Bake at 325 degrees for 1 hour and 15 minutes or until cake tests done.

Mama's Pound Cake

Mrs. Laura Newbury, whose daughter Mrs. Maxine Reese says, "I guarantee it is the best thing you ever tasted."

1 cup vegetable shortening plus 2 tablespoons
2 cups sugar
2 cups plain flour

6 eggs
1 teaspoon vanilla

Cream together shortening and sugar; add eggs one at a time, mixing well after each. Blend in flour and vanilla, mix well. Pour into a greased and floured tube pan. Place in a cold oven. Turn oven on to 325 degrees and bake one hour. Do not open oven door during that time.

If desired, add ½ teaspoon mace and ½ teaspoon lemon extract in place of vanilla or 1 teaspoon butter flavoring in place of vanilla.

There is no liquid in the recipe.

Elegant Pound Cake

8 eggs, separated
2⅔ cups sugar
1 pound butter (no substitute)
3½ cups sifted cake flour
½ teaspoon salt
½ cup coffee cream
1 teaspoon vanilla

Separate eggs. Measure sugar and set aside. Beat egg whites until soft peaks form; gradually add 6 tablespoons of the sugar while continuing to beat until stiff. Refrigerate until needed.

In large mixer bowl cream butter; gradually add remaining sugar. Beat in well-beaten egg yolks. Sift flour and salt together three times and add alternately with cream and vanilla to creamed mixture. Beat until mixture is very light. Fold in egg whites by hand; pour into greased and floured 10-inch tube pan at least 4 inches deep. Bake in a 300-degree oven for 1¾ hours or until cake tests done. Invert on rack and allow to cool. Loosen around edges and remove to serving plate. Requires no icing. If desired, dribble on a powdered sugar glaze. Serves 15 to 18. Freezes well.

Deep Chocolate Cake

5 plain milk chocolate bars, 1⅜ oz. each
1½ cans (1 lb. or 16 oz. each) chocolate syrup
2 teaspoons vanilla
2 sticks (1 cup) butter or margarine
2 cups sugar
4 eggs
½ teaspoon soda
2½ cups plain flour, unsifted
1 cup buttermilk
1 cup pecans, chopped

Preheat oven to 350 degrees. Melt candy and syrup in top of double boiler over boiling water. Add vanilla and set aside to cool. Cream butter or margarine and sugar. Add eggs, one at a time; add chocolate mixture and blend. Stir soda and flour together; add to creamed mixture alternately with buttermilk. Add nuts. Turn batter into large tube pan or bundt pan. Bake for 1 to 1½ hours or until cake tests done.

—*Sara Spano*

Hot Milk Cake

4 eggs
2 cups sugar
1 teaspoon vanilla
2 cups unsifted plain flour
2 teaspoons baking powder
Pinch of salt
1 cup milk
1 stick butter or margarine

Beat eggs until light and lemon colored gradually adding sugar and continue beating. Add vanilla. Meanwhile, sift together flour, baking powder and salt. Heat milk and butter or margarine together until milk is hot and butter is melted. Add flour mixture to creamed mixture and blend. Stir in hot milk and butter. Blend together quickly and pour into two greased and floured 9-inch cake pans lined with waxed paper. Bake in a 375 degree oven for 25 minutes or until cake tests done.

Turn out of pans onto wire racks. Peel off waxed paper and allow to cool. Frost and coat frosting with coconut.

FROSTING

¾ cup sugar
⅓ cup white corn syrup
2 tablespoons water
¼ teaspoon cream of tartar
¼ teaspoon salt
2 egg whites
1 teaspoon vanilla

Combine all ingredients except vanilla in top of double boiler. Place over boiling water and beat constantly with electric mixer for five minutes or until soft peaks are formed. The frosting looks like the whitest of cold cream and spreads on the cake the way you might think a cloud would spread. Enough for center and outside of two nine-inch layers. To make fresh coconut cake, coat outside generously with fresh coconut.

To make coconut easier to remove from shell, after cracking, place pieces in a 350 degree oven for about 10 minutes.

Fresh Coconut Cake

¾ cup vegetable shortening
1½ cups vegetable shortening
3 cups cake flour
4 teaspoons baking powder
¼ teaspoon salt
1 teaspoon vanilla
1 cup milk
5 egg whites

Cream together shortening and sugar. Sift flour, baking powder and salt; add alternately with milk to creamed mixture. Add vanilla and fold in stiffly beaten egg whites. Pour into two greased and floured 9-inch layer cake pans. Bake in a 375 degree oven for 30 minutes or until done. Cool and spread with this filling.

FILLING

2½ cups sugar
2½ tablespoons flour
2 cups milk
Pinch of baking soda
1 teaspoon vanilla
2 fresh coconuts, finely grated

Combine sugar and flour; add milk, soda and butter. Cook, stirring, until mixture thickens. Remove from heat; add vanilla and coconut.

—Virginia Williams

My Grandmother Harris'
Lady Baltimore Cake

Virginia Williams: "This is a real old recipe—and is very rich—sometimes I just use any yellow cake batter recipe such as the 1-2-3-4 cake and then use the Lady Baltimore filling."

CAKE BATTER:

1⅔ cups butter
1½ cups sugar
3 cups cake flour
4 teaspoons baking powder
1 cup milk
4 egg yolks
1 whole egg

Cream together butter and sugar. Sift together flour, baking powder and add alternately with milk and eggs to creamed mixture gradually. Bake in two greased and floured layer cake pans in a 350 degree oven for 30 minutes or until done.

FILLING

2½ cups sugar
Pinch of soda
2½ tablespoons flour
2 cups milk
½ cup butter
2 cups finely grated coconut
1 cup seeded muscat raisins, cut fine
1 cup chopped pecans

Put soda in sugar; stir in flour. Combine in a saucepan with milk and butter. Let mixture cool, stirring, until smooth and thick enough so it will stay on cake. Remove from heat; add coconut, raisins and pecans. Spread on cake.

Atlanta Lane Cake

1 cup butter or margarine
2 cups sugar
3½ cups cake flour, sifted
2 teaspoons baking powder
½ teaspoon salt
1 cup milk
1 teaspoon vanilla
8 egg whites, stiffly beaten

Cream butter and sugar together until light and fluffy. Sift together dry ingredients and add to creamed mixture alternately with milk and vanilla, beginning and ending with dry ingredients. Fold in egg whites. Pour into 3 8-inch layer cake pans which have been greased and floured and the bottoms lined with greased and floured brown paper. Bake in a 375-degree oven for 25 to 30 minutes or until cake tests done. Turn out on racks to cool. When cool, fill and top with Lane filling (recipe below).

LANE FILLING

- ½ cup butter or margarine
- 1 cup sugar
- 8 egg yolks
- 1 cup seeded raisins, chopped
- 1 cup nuts, chopped
- 2 teaspoons brandy or rum extract

Cream butter and sugar together. Beat egg yolks and add. Cook over hot water, stirring, until thick. Add remaining ingredients. Cool. Spread between layers and on top of cake.

Spice Cake

½ pound butter
½ cup shortening
3 cups sugar
5 eggs
3 cups flour, sifted
½ teaspoon mace
½ teaspoon allspice
¼ teaspoon nutmeg
½ teaspoon cloves
½ teaspoon salt
½ teaspoon baking powder
1 cup plus 2 tablespoons milk
½ teaspoon vanilla

Cream butter, shortening, and sugar until light and fluffy. Add eggs, one at a time, continue to cream. Sift together twice the flour, spices, salt, and baking powder. Add to creamed mixture alternately with milk. Add vanilla. Turn into a large greased and floured tube pan. Bake in a 325-degree oven for 1 hour and 15 minutes or until cake tests done.

Sweet Potato Layer Cake

1½ cups cooking oil
2 cups sugar
4 eggs, separated
4 tablespoons hot water
2½ cups sifted cake flour

3 teaspoons baking powder
¼ teaspoon salt
1 teaspoon ground cinnamon
1 teaspoon nutmeg
1½ cups grated North Carolina sweet potatoes (yams)
1 cup chopped nuts
1 teaspoon vanilla

Combine cooking oil, sugar and beat well until smooth, add egg yolks and beat well. Add hot water, then dry ingredients which have been sifted together. Stir in sweet potatoes, nuts and vanilla, beat well. Beat egg whites until stiff and fold into mixture. Bake in 3 greased 8-inch cake pans lined with greased and floured brown paper cut from grocery bags in a 350-degree oven for 25 to 30 minutes or until cake tests done. Cool and frost (recipe below).

SWEET POTATO CAKE FROSTING

1 can (14½ oz.) evaporated milk
1 cup sugar
½ cup (1 stick) margarine
3 egg yolks
1 teaspoon vanilla
1⅓ cups flaked coconut

Combine milk, sugar, margarine, egg yolks and vanilla in top of double boiler. Cook 12 minutes until thick, stirring constantly until mixture thickens, remove from heat and add coconut. Beat until cool and frost cake.

Date Pecan Cake

1 cup flour
1 teaspoon baking powder
⅛ teaspoon salt
1 cup sugar
1 pound dates, diced
1 heaping quart pecan halves
½ pound butter, melted
1 teaspoon vanilla
4 eggs, separated

Sift flour, baking powder, salt, and sugar over dates and
pecans; mix in butter and vanilla. Beat egg yolks; add and
mix well. Beat egg whites until stiff; fold in gently. Pour
into a greased tube pan lined with greased and floured
brown paper. Bake at 275 degrees for 1 hour and 15
minutes or until done. Cool in pan.

Prune Cake with Buttermilk Icing

The ingredients in this recipe may sound a little odd
but it evermore makes a luscious melt-in-the-mouth
cake.

1½ cups granulated sugar
1 cup vegetable oil
3 eggs
1 teaspoon vanilla
2 cups sifted flour
1 teaspoon soda

1 teaspoon cinnamon
1 teaspoon nutmeg
1 teaspoon allspice
¼ teaspoon salt
1 cup buttermilk
1 cup chopped nuts
1 cup cooked, pitted, chopped prunes

Blend sugar and oil. Add eggs, one at a time and mix well. Add vanilla. Sift flour with soda, spices and salt. Add to egg mixture alternately with buttermilk, blending well after each addition. Add nuts and prunes.

Pour into a greased pan—it just fits into one 11 × 8 inches and 2 inches deep. Bake at 325 degrees for 1 hour or until it tests done.

BUTTERMILK ICING

1 cup granulated sugar
½ cup buttermilk
½ teaspoon soda
1 tablespoon light corn syrup
¼ cup butter
½ teaspoon vanilla

Mix all ingredients together in a deep pan—otherwise it will boil over. Stir over low heat until sugar is dissolved. Continue cooking, without stirring, to the soft boil stage.

Pour mixture over hot cake without beating. Spread evenly. Leave the cake in the pan until ready to cut into blocks for serving. Because it is a tender cake, it will break otherwise.

Graham Cracker Cake

1 pound Graham crackers
½ pound butter
2 cups sugar
5 eggs
2 teaspoons baking powder
1 can flaked coconut
1 cup chopped pecans
1 No. 2 can crushed pineapple well drained
1 cup milk

Roll Graham crackers to make crumbs. Cream butter and add sugar gradually, creaming both until light and fluffy. Add eggs, one at a time beating well after each addition.

Blend baking powder into crumbs and add to creamed mixture alternately with milk. Add coconut, nuts and well drained pineapple. Blend.

Grease and line the bottoms of two 9-inch layer cake pans 1¼ inches deep—grease and flour paper, too. Pour in cake batter. Bake in a 350 degree oven for 35 to 40 minutes or until cake shrinks from the sides of the pans. Remove from oven and let stand 5 minutes before turning out.

Cool and frost as desired. I used caramel frosting.

Super Shortcake

2 cups self-rising flour
2 tablespoons sugar
¼ cup shortening

1 cup whipping cream
Blueberry filling or sauce or other fruit

Stir together flour and sugar. Cut in shortening until mixture resembles coarse crumbs. Reserve ¼ cup cream. Add ¾ cup cream to flour mixture. Stir quickly to make a soft dough (I found about 2 to 3 tablespoons buttermilk were required to make a dough of the proper consistency.) Press into a ball. Pat out on a greased baking sheet to a round about 9 inches in diameter or roll out on lightly floured surface to about ¾ inch thick. Cut out 2 biscuits with 4½ to 5-inch floured round cutter. Press remaining dough to make third biscuit.

Place on lightly greased baking sheet. Bake in a 425 degree oven 12 to 15 minutes or until lightly browned. Cool slightly. Split and fill with blueberry filling—the canned pie filling is a short cut or use other fruit as desired. Top with more filling, lemon sherbet or vanilla ice cream and garnish with remaining whipped cream.

Blackberry Roll

> **2 cups flour, sifted**
> **2 teaspoons baking powder**
> **1 teaspoon salt**
> **2 tablespoons sugar**
> **⅓ cup plus 4 tablespoons butter**
> **1 egg**
> **⅓ cup milk, approximate**
> **1 pint of blackberries sweetened with ⅔ to ¾ cup sugar**

Sift together flour, baking powder, salt and sugar. Cut in ⅓ cup butter with pastry blender or two knives until mixture resembles crumbs. Beat egg; add with sufficient milk to make soft dough; mix lightly. Turn out on lightly floured board and knead just enough to make the dough cling together. Roll out to a thickness of about ¼ inch. Spread with remaining soft butter. Cover with sweetened blackberries. Roll up like a jelly roll. It is a good idea to roll the dough on wax paper, as the dough is tender and rich and difficult to lift into the baking pan. Lifting wax paper, turn over into baking pan. Bake in a 400-degree oven for 25 minutes or until golden brown. Cut into slices and serve warm with berry sauce or thick cream. Makes 6 to 8 servings.

BERRY SAUCE

The sauce is similar to hot blackberry jam.

1 cup blackberries
¾ cup sugar
Juice of ½ lemon

Blend all ingredients and cook over medium heat, stirring, until clear like jam. Add a small amount of water if needed.

Crisp Sugar Cookies

½ cup (1 stick) butter or margarine
½ cup shortening
1½ cups sugar
2½ cups sifted flour
½ teaspoon soda
⅓ teaspoon salt
1 egg
2 tablespoons vinegar

1 teaspoon vanilla
Sugar

Cream together butter or margarine and sugar. Sift together dry ingredients and add alternately to creamed mixture with egg blended with vinegar and vanilla.

Shape dough into small balls. Place on ungreased baking sheet. Mash down with glass dipped in sugar. Bake in a 400 degree oven for 8 to 10 minutes or until lightly browned. Immediately upon removing from oven, run a sharp knife under the cookies. Makes about 6 dozen.

Oatmeal Lace Cookies

There is no flour in the recipe.

1 egg, beaten
1 cup dark brown sugar, packed
1 teaspoon vanilla
½ cup melted margarine
2½ cups quick oats, uncooked
2 teaspoons double acting baking powder

Beat egg. Add sugar, vanilla, margarine and mix. Add baking powder to oats and add to egg mixture. Blend well. The mixture will be almost crumbly.

Drop by the half teaspoon onto a greased baking sheet allowing room to spread. Bake 10 minutes or until browned in 350 degree oven. Run a spatula under the cookies when they come from the oven, otherwise they will stick.

To make oatmeal cooky sandwiches, drop 2 or 3

teaspoons of the mixture on the baking sheet. Bake and put two cookies together with butter cream filling.

Make butter cream filling by blending one-third cup soft butter with 1 cup sifted confectioners' sugar and 1 teaspoon vanilla.

Chess Cookies

½ cup butter
2 cups brown sugar, packed
2 eggs
1½ cups flour, sifted
2 teaspoons baking powder
⅛ teaspoon salt
1 cup nuts, chopped
1 teaspoon vanilla

Melt butter in heavy skillet; add brown sugar, heat over low heat, stirring, until sugar is melted and bubbles. Remove from heat; cool to lukewarm. Blend in eggs, one at a time. Sift together flour, baking powder, and salt; blend into creamed mixture. Add nuts and vanilla. Pour into greased 8-inch-square baking pan; bake in 350 degree oven for 30 to 35 minutes. The cookies puff during baking and sink slightly when cool. Cut into squares. Makes 25 squares.

Fabulous Fudge Squares

1½ cups sifted flour
¼ teaspoon salt
1 teaspoon baking powder

⅔ cup butter or margarine
3 squares (1 ounce each) unsweetened chocolate,
    melted
2 cups granulated sugar
3 eggs, beaten
⅓ cup milk
2 teaspoons vanilla
1 cup chopped pecans

Sift flour with salt and baking powder. Add butter to chocolate and blend. Combine sugar and eggs; add chocolate mixture, beating thoroughly. Alternate flour mixture and milk, then vanilla and nuts.

Pour into greased pan 9 by 13 by 2 inches. Bake in a 350 degree oven about 35 minutes or until done. Cut into squares before removing from pan.

Lemon Squares

1½ cups sifted flour
½ teaspoon salt
¼ teaspoon baking powder
3 eggs, separated
1 cup confectioners' sugar
½ cup butter
1 cup sugar
2 tablespoons grated lemon rind
⅓ cup lemon juice

Sift together flour, salt and baking powder. Beat egg whites until soft mounds begin to form. Add confectioners' sugar, gradually and continue beating until stiff peaks are formed.

Cream butter; add sugar and cream well together. Add egg yolks, one at a time, and beat well after each. Add lemon juice alternately with dry ingredients. Blend well. Add lemon rind and fold in egg whites gently but thoroughly. Pour into a greased and floured pan about 11 by 7 inches. Bake in a 350 degree oven 25 minutes or until done.

While still warm, spread frosting. To make frosting, blend together 1 cup confectioners' sugar, 1 tablespoon cream and 2 tablespoons soft butter with enough hot water to make of spreading consistency. Cut into squares.

Scotch Bars

1 12-oz. package chocolate pieces
1 15-oz. can sweetened condensed milk
2 tablespoons butter or margarine
1 cup butter or margarine, melted
1 lb. box or 2¼ cups firmly packed brown sugar
2 eggs
2 cups all purpose flour
1 teaspoon vanilla
1 teaspoon salt
1 cup chopped pecans
½ cup flaked coconut

In top of double boiler, melt chocolate pieces with milk and 2 tablespoons butter. Blend until smooth. Set aside.

In large mixing bowl, combine melted butter, brown sugar and eggs. No need to sift flour; measure by lightly spooning into cup and leveling off. Add flour and salt; blend well. Stir in vanilla, pecans and coconut; mix well. Spread half of dough in ungreased jelly roll pan. Drizzle chocolate mixture over dough in pan. Dot top of chocolate mixture with remaining brown sugar dough. Swirl slightly with tip of knife. Bake at 350 degrees for 30 to

35 minutes or until dough is golden brown. Cool; cut into bars. Makes about 48 bars.

Persimmon Pudding

1 cup soft butter
2 cups sugar
3 pints of persimmon pulp
4 eggs, beaten
1½ cups self-rising flour
½ teaspoon cinnamon
½ teaspoon cloves
½ teaspoon allspice
1 teaspoon vanilla
½ cup corn meal
2 cups grated raw sweet potatoes
3 cups sweet milk

Cream butter and sugar together. Add persimmon pulp and eggs and blend well. Sift flour with spices and add with corn meal to cream mixture alternately with milk. Add sweet potatoes.

Pour into a buttered baking dish and bake at 350 degrees for one hour, stirring thoroughly four times as the mixture bakes.

To substitute regular all purpose flour for self-rising, use 1½ cups and add 2 teaspoons baking powder and ½ teaspoon salt.

The pudding is best served warm with whipped cream.

Trifle

This is the way Martha Washington, the nation's First Lady made trifle.

Sponge cake, Naples biscuit, or jelly roll cut into slices
½ cup white wine, sherry or brandy
1 pint whipping cream
1 tablespoon sugar
Rich custard, recipe follows
Candied fruits and angelica for decoration

Line the bottom and sides of a deep dish with slices of sponge cake, Naples biscuit, or jelly roll. Wet them with ⅓ cup wine, and fill the dish nearly to the top with rich boiled custard. Season ½ pint heavy cream with one tablespoon wine and one tablespoon sugar; whip it to a froth and lay it on the custard. Cover and decorate with the remaining ½ pint of whipped cream, preserves of any kind, candied fruits and angelica.

RICH CUSTARD

1 quart milk, scalded
½ cup cold milk
½ cup sugar
Pinch salt
6 eggs
¼ teaspoon vanilla or almond extract

Scald one quart milk; add ½ cup sugar, and a pinch of salt. Beat six whole eggs and add cold milk to them. Stir, and gradually add to the hot milk mixture. Cook in top of double boiler until custard coats the spoon. When cold, add the flavoring.

Banana Pudding

Banana pudding evolved from trifle, another of Martha Washington's favorites and a favorite for centuries in England.

To make banana pudding of the kind that was bountiful on the dessert table at the Million Dollar Supper, and the kind the people of Plains like, omit the wine, use vanilla wafers, add layers of sliced bananas and top all with meringue. That kind of banana pudding is significant for the same reason marshmallows and Jello were in meals, because bananas and vanilla wafers, about 1/3 of the twelve ounce package that sells today for 65 cents, was 5 cents in the 1930s.

The recipe from the Nabisco box is the one cooks use today.

About every fourth of fifth space on the dessert table at the supper was filled with a banana pudding, a great favorite in Plains. In discussing the supper several days after it, Mrs. P. J. Wise said, "I made a banana pudding about this big," and held her hands out to indicate a pudding three or four times the usual recipe.

Superb Boiled Custard

4 egg yolks or 2 whole eggs, beaten
⅓ cup sugar
¼ teaspoon salt
1½ cups scalded milk
½ teaspoon almond extract
1 teaspoon vanilla extract

Blend eggs, sugar, and salt. Stir in hot milk gradually. Mix well and set over simmering water, or use a heavy saucepan over low heat. Stirring constantly, cook until mixture coats spoon thinly. Pour immediately into a chilled bowl, or place saucepan in a pan of ice water. Add extracts. Refrigerate covered until serving time.

Bread Pudding

1 1-pound loaf bread or equivalent, coarsely broken
1 quart milk hot
3 eggs, beaten
2 cups sugar
2 tablespoons vanilla
1 cup golden raisins
3 tablespoons margarine

Pour hot milk over bread in bowl. Blend eggs, sugar and vanilla; add to bread and mix well. Add raisins. In 9 × 13 baking pan, melt margarine; pour mixture into pan. Bake in a 350-degree oven for 40 minutes or until firm and

golden brown. Makes 24 servings. Serve warm or cold
with nutmeg or lemon sauce (recipes below).

NUTMEG SAUCE

1 tablespoon flour
½ cup sugar
1 cup water, boiling
1 egg, beaten
½ teaspoon nutmeg

In saucepan, blend flour and sugar; add boiling water.
Cook, stirring, until smooth and thick. Pour a small
amount of hot liquid into egg; beat together and add remaining hot liquid. Return to heat; cook 1 minute longer.
Remove from heat; add nutmeg. Serve warm. Makes
about 1 cup.

LEMON SAUCE

½ cup sugar
1 tablespoon cornstarch or 2 tablespoons flour
1 teaspoon lemon rind, grated
1 cup water
2 tablespoons butter or margarine
2 tablespoons lemon juice

In saucepan, blend sugar, cornstarch, and lemon rind; stir
in cold water and cook until clear and thick, stirring constantly. Remove from heat; stir in butter and lemon juice
until butter is melted. Serve hot or cold. Makes about 1
cup.

Sweet Potato Custard Pie

1 cup mashed cooked sweet potatoes
¼ cup melted butter
¾ cup brown sugar
3 eggs
1½ cups milk
Dash to ¼ teaspoon each of nutmeg, cinnamon
    and cloves
Pastry

Add butter to sweet potatoes. Separate eggs. Beat yolks with sugar. Add potatoes, milk and spices. Beat egg whites until stiff and fold into mixture. Pour into unbaked pie shell which has been brushed with slightly beaten egg white and then allowed to stand for a while—this helps prevent sogginess.

Bake in a 350 degree oven until mixture is set and lightly browned.

Sliced Sweet Potato Pie

Line a deep pie dish (one which is 1½ to 2 inches deep) with unbaked pastry. Peel raw sweet potatoes and slice as thinly as possible—that means real thin. Fill pastry with potato slices, sprinkle layers with sugar (use either brown or white as you prefer), dust with cinnamon and dot with butter. Add a sprinkle of salt here and there and dribble 1 teaspoon vanilla over the top layer.

Dot top layer liberally with butter. Top with gashed top crust.

For a golden crust, brush with slightly beaten egg white. Bake in a 350 degree oven for one hour or until done. To test for doneness, stick a knife down through the pie. If potatoes are done, knife will slip in easily. It is best served slightly warm.

Coconut Macaroon Pie

2 eggs
1½ cups sugar
½ teaspoon salt
½ cup soft butter
¼ cup flour
½ cup milk
1 teaspoon vanilla
1½ cups shredded coconut
1 9-inch pie shell, unbaked

Beat eggs, adding sugar gradually until lemon colored. Beat in salt. Add butter and flour and blend well. Add milk and vanilla. Fold in 1 cup coconut. Pour into unbaked pie shell and sprinkle with remaining ½ cup coconut. Bake in a 325-degree oven for 1 hour or until done and top is browned.

Brown Sugar Pie

½ cup (1 stick) butter
2 cups brown sugar, packed
3 eggs
1 teaspoon vanilla
Pastry

Cream butter. Add sugar and cream well together. Add unbeaten eggs, one at a time, and blend well but do not beat more than absolutely necessary. Add vanilla and pour mixture into a 9-inch pie pan lined with unbaked pastry.

Bake at 450 degrees for 5 minutes. Reduce temperature to 325 degrees and bake 25 minutes longer or until filling is firm.

Lemon Custard Pie

You have a lovely treat in store with this recipe.

2 cups sugar
2 tablespoons corn meal
1 tablespoon flour
4 eggs, unbeaten
¼ melted butter
¼ cup milk
¼ cup lemon juice
4 teaspoons grated lemon rind
Unbaked pastry.

Mix sugar, corn meal and flour. Add eggs, one at a time, and beat well after each. Stir in butter, milk, lemon juice and rind and mix well.

Pour mixture into pie pan lined with unbaked pastry. Place on lower shelf of oven and bake at 350 degrees for 45 minutes or until firm. Allow to cool before cutting.

Butterscotch Pie

1 cup brown sugar, firmly packed
3 tablespoons water
1 tablespoon butter
Pinch of salt
⅛ teaspoon soda
½ cup flour
1½ cups of cold water
3 eggs, separated
6 tablespoons sugar

Add water, butter and salt to brown sugar. Bring to a boil and remove from heat while adding soda to keep it from bubbling over. Cook to the hard ball stage.

Meanwhile, blend the flour with some of the milk to make smooth paste, gradually adding remaining milk. Add to beaten egg yolks and cook together over boiling water, stirring constantly, until smooth and thick.

Pour hot brown sugar mixture into flour mixture and beat well to blend. Cool just slightly and pour into cooled prepared crust.

Make meringue with 3 egg whites. Beat until foamy and begin adding sugar gradually and continue beating until shiny and mixture stands in stiff peaks. Spread to edge of crust and twirl on top. Brown at 375 degrees.

Rhubarb Pie

1¾ cups sugar
½ cup plus 3 tablespoons flour
⅜ teaspoon salt
¼ cup butter or margarine
2 tablespoons butter or margarine, melted
1 egg, beaten
4 cups fresh rhubarb, cut in slices about ½ inch thick
1 9-inch pastry shell, unbaked

Blend ½ cup sugar, ½ cup flour, and ⅛ teaspoon salt for the topping. Cut in ¼ cup butter until mixture is like coarse cornmeal. Set aside while making pie. Combine remaining 1¼ cups sugar, 3 tablespoons flour, ¼ teaspoon salt, melted butter, egg, and rhubarb, and turn into pastry shell. Sprinkle with topping. Bake at 425 degrees for about 40 minutes or until filling bubbles up and pastry is brown. If topping and pastry brown too fast, reduce heat to 375 degrees to complete cooking.

Peach Crumble Pie

6 cups sliced peeled peaches
1 cup sugar
3 tablespoons cornstarch
⅛ teaspoon salt
1 egg
½ teaspoon almond extract
Unbaked pastry-lined deep 9 or 10-inch pie pan
Topping, recipe follows

Mix sugar, cornstarch and salt; add beaten egg and almond extract; pour over peaches. Mix together gently. Turn into pie shell. Sprinkle with topping. Bake in a 375 degree oven until bubbly and golden brown, about 25 minutes.

TOPPING

½ **cup flour**
½ **cup sugar**
½ **stick (¼ cup butter)**

Blend flour and sugar; cut in butter until finely crumbled.

Peach Upside Down Pie

1 **12-inch square aluminum foil**
2 **tablespoons butter, soft**
⅔ **cup toasted pecan halves**
9 **tablespoons brown sugar**
Pastry for double-crust 9-inch pie, unbaked
5 **cups (about 8 medium) fresh peaches, peeled and sliced**
¾ **cup granulated sugar**
2 **tablespoons quick-cooking tapioca**
½ **teaspoon nutmeg**
¼ **teaspoon cinnamon**
1 **egg white, slightly beaten**

Line a 9-inch pie pan with foil; let excess foil overhang edge. Spread butter on bottom of foil; press nuts and 5 tablespoons brown sugar into butter. Fit a layer of pastry over nuts and brown sugar in pie pan. Mix peaches with granulated sugar, 4 tablespoons brown sugar, tapioca, and spices; pour into pastry shell. Cover with another layer of pastry, pricked to allow steam to escape; seal and flute edges. Brush with egg white. Bake in 450 degree oven for 10 minutes; lower heat to 375 degrees, and bake 35 to 40 minutes longer or until done. Turn out upside down.

Deep Dish Peach Pie

    1 tablespoon flour
    1 cup sugar
    8 large peaches, peeled and sliced
    ½ teaspoon nutmeg
    ¼ cup butter
    Pastry for double-crust pie 9-inch pie rolled ⅛-inch
        thick
    Vanilla ice cream or whipped cream

Cut pastry into strips 1-inch wide. In botton of deep 9-inch-square baking dish, crisscross ⅓ of the pastry strips. Blend flour and 1 tablespoon sugar; sprinkle over strips. Add half the peaches; sprinkle with half of remaining sugar. Dot with half the butter. Crisscross with another third of pastry strips. Add remaining peaches and sugar, sprinkle with nutmeg, dot with remaining butter. Crisscross with remaining pastry strips. Bake in a 450-degree oven for 15 minutes; reduce temperature to 350 degrees, and bake 20 minutes longer. Serve warm with scoop of ice cream or mounds of whipped cream. Makes 8 to 10 servings.

Fried Peach Pies

Also called half moon pies.

1 11-ounce package dried peaches
Water
½ cup sugar
1 9½-ounce carton ready-to-bake biscuits
Lard

Place peaches with water to cover in saucepan; simmer for 30 minutes or until soft. Drain off excess liquid; discard. Mash peaches with potato masher; add sugar, cool thoroughly. Roll out biscuits on lightly floured board to make thin circles about 6 inches in diameter. Place portion of peach mixture on one half of each circle; fold over other half, seal edge tightly with a fork. Brown on each side in about ¼ inch hot lard in a heavy skillet. Makes 10.

Fresh Peach Cake

½ cup butter
1½ cups brown sugar, packed
1 egg
2 cups sifted flour
1 teaspoon soda
⅛ teaspoon salt
1 cup buttermilk
4 peaches, peeled and diced
¼ cup white sugar
1 teaspoon cinnamon

Cream butter with brown sugar. Add egg and continue to cream. Sift together flour, soda and salt and add to creamed mixture alternately with buttermilk. Blend. Fold in peaches. Pour batter into greased baking pan 13 by 9 inches. Mix white sugar and cinnamon and sprinkle over the top. Bake in a 350 degree oven for 30 to 35 minutes or until done.

Peach Kuchen

2 cups flour, sifted
¼ teaspoon baking powder
½ teaspoon salt
1 cup sugar
½ cup butter or margarine
12 fresh peach halves, peeled
¼ teaspoon nutmeg
¼ teaspoon cardamom
2 egg yolks
1 cup heavy or sour cream

Sift together four, baking powder, salt, and 2 tablespoons sugar; cut in butter or margarine until mixture resembles coarse cornmeal. Spread and pat in an even layer over the bottom and up a portion of the sides of an 8-inch-square pan. Arrange peaches, cut side up, on pastry; sprinkle peaches with mixture of remaining sugar, nutmeg, and cardamom. Bake in a 400-degree oven for 15 minutes; mix egg yolks and cream, pour over peaches. Bake 30 minutes longer. Makes 9 servings.

Fresh Peach Nut Bread

4 eggs
2 cups granulated sugar
1 cup salad oil
3½ cups unsifted flour
1 teaspoon cinnamon
¾ teaspoon baking powder
1½ teaspoons salt
1½ teaspoons baking soda
2½ cups diced, firm ripe peaches
1 teaspoon vanilla
1 cup chopped pecans

Lightly grease and flour three disposable foil loaf pans 8 by 4 by 2¼ inches. Chop nuts; set aside.

Beat eggs; gradually beat in sugar, then oil and vanilla. Sift in dry ingredients; add to first mixture alternately with half of diced peaches. Fold in remaining peaches and nuts. Pour into loaf pans and bake on second lowest rack of 350 degree oven for 45 minutes to 55 minutes or until done. Makes three loaves.

Frozen Peach Torte

1⅓ cups fine graham cracker crumbs
⅓ cup melted butter
2 eggs
¼ cup lemon juice
½ cup sugar
⅛ teaspoon grated lemon rind
1½ cups chopped fresh peaches
½ cup whipped whipping cream

Blend crumbs and butter together; sprinkle half the mixture in bottom of refrigerator tray. Beat egg yolks lightly, add lemon juice, sugar and salt and cook and stir over hot water until slightly thickened. Remove from heat and blend in rind. Cool.

Beat egg whites until slightly thickened. Remove from heat and blend in rind. Cool.

Beat egg whites until stiff. Whip cream until stiff. Fold peaches, beaten egg whites and cream into cooled lemon mixture. Pour over crumbs in tray. Sprinkle top with remaining crumbs. Place in freezing compartment and freeze with control set at lowest temperature. Makes 6 to 8 servings.

Peach Ice Cream

    1 **quart fresh peaches, crushed and peeled**
    1½ **cups sugar**
    ½ **pint light cream**
    ½ **pint heavy cream**
    1 **quart milk**
    1 **tablespoon vanilla extract**
    1 **teaspoon almond extract**

Combine peaches and sugar, mixing well. Let stand for 10 minutes. Add light and heavy cream, milk and extracts.

Pour into freezer can, filling ⅔ full.

Pack freezer with 1 cup ice cream salt to each 8 cups crushed ice in alternate layers. Turn until frozen. Pack down to ripen. Makes 1 gallon.

Peach Yummy

3 cups sliced fresh peaches
1 cup granulated sugar
1 teaspoon cinnamon
¾ cup brown sugar
¾ cup rolled oats
½ cup flour
½ teaspoon soda
½ teaspoon baking powder
½ teaspoon salt
½ cup butter

Place peaches, granulated sugar and cinnamon in bottom of greased deep baking dish.

Blend together remaining ingredients until crumbly. Sprinkle over peaches and bake in a 400 degree oven for 30 to 40 minutes or until browned. Serve topped with ice cream or whipped cream.

Peach Leather

2½ cups ripe peach pulp, mashed
½ cup sugar plus sugar for sprinkling

Combine pulp and sugar in heavy skillet; cook, stirring, until thickened. Spread out in a thin layer on oiled baking sheet; cover with mosquito netting and gauze, and place in the hot sun to dry for 3 days, bringing it inside at night. When the leather draws away from the pan, it is done. Place on board sprinkled with sugar, and sprinkle sugar over the top. Roll out as thin as a knife blade, then cut into strips 1½ inches wide. Make small wafer and roll up; dust again with sugar. Store in tin box with tight lid.

Peanuts

Near the end of the primaries, when it became apparent that Jimmy Carter's campaign was more than "just peanuts"—the expression used for something meager—books about peanuts and peanut butter began to appear.

In Plains, Ga., the growing of peanuts is their major agricultural industry. Peanuts there are what corn is to Iowa, cheese is to Wisconsin, and grapes to France.

Jimmy Carter Cocktail

Soon after the election, in the wake of the continued attention paid to the peanut, Vic Cappelle of a restaurant in Fond Du Lac, Wis., composed a drink named a "Jimmy Carter." It is made of one ounce of white creme de cacao, an ounce of liquor—whiskey, brandy, bourbon or scotch— a teaspoon of creamy peanut butter and a small scoop of crushed ice blended together.

Salted Peanuts

These are the peanuts Virginia Williams (Mrs. Frank) keeps on hand at the peanut company where she serves to whoever comes.

3 pints peanut cooking oil
1 quart raw unshelled peanuts

Heat oil in deep fat fryer to 400 degrees. Put peanuts in basket and cook, uncovered 4 to 5 minutes. Pour out on tray lined with paper towel. Salt to taste. Will keep several days in covered jar.

This oil can be used to do several quarts of peanuts.

Peanut Butter

The old way was to grind peanuts several times in the meat grinder. This way should prove faster.

2 cups peanuts, roasted and salted
2 to 3 tablespoons peanut oil

Combine peanuts and oil in electric blender. Blend until smooth. Makes 1 cup.

Peanut Butter Balls

½ cup crunchy nut peanut butter
⅔ cup sweetened condensed milk
1¾ cup sifted confectioner's sugar
1 cup seedless raisins
1 teaspoon grated lemon rind

Combine all ingredients and blend well. Chill slightly and then shape into balls about one inch in diameter. Roll balls in additional sifted confectioners' sugar. Makes about 36 balls.

Crunchy Peanut Logs

1 cup peanut butter
⅔ cup sifted powdered sugar
⅓ cup instant non-fat dry milk powder
⅓ cup finely chopped peanuts
2 tablespoons water
1 tablespoon corn syrup
½ cup flaked coconut

In a mixing bowl combine peanut butter, powdered sugar, non-fat dry milk powder, peanuts, water and corn syrup. Shape into two logs 8 inches long and 1½ inches thick. Roll in coconut. Chill until firm. Cut into 36 slices.

Chocolate Peanut Candy

1 cup peanut butter, creamy or chunk style
1 cup corn syrup, light or dark
½ cup cocoa
1¼ cups powdered skim milk
1¼ cups sifted confectioners' sugar

Blend peanut butter and syrup. Add cocoa and blend. Add powdered milk and sugar all at once. Mix together, first with a spoon and then knead with the hands.

Turn out on board and continue kneading until mixture is well blended and smooth. Press out with hands or rolling pin into squares a half inch thick. Cut into squares. Top with nuts, if desired. Makes about 2 pounds.

Peanut Brittle

President Carter's favorite.

3 cups sugar
1½ cups water
1 cup white Karo syrup
3 cups raw peanuts
2 tablespoons soda
½ stick butter
1 teaspoon vanilla

Boil sugar, water and Karo until it spins a thread; add peanuts. After adding peanuts, stir constantly until syrup turns golden brown. Remove from heat; adding remaining ingredients; stir until butter melts. Pour out quickly on 2 cookie sheets with sides. As mixture begins to harden around edges, pull until thin.

Peanut Brittle II

½ cup light corn syrup
2 cups granulated sugar
½ cup brown sugar
½ cup water
¼ cup butter
⅛ teaspoon salt
⅛ teaspoon soda
1½ cups peanuts

Combine syrup, sugars, water, and butter in top of double boiler or deep saucepan; cook, stirring occasionally, to 270 degrees F. Continue cooking, stirring more frequently, to 300 degrees F. Remove from heat; stir salt, soda, and peanuts in quickly. Pour onto buttered baking sheet; stretch out thin, and cool. Break into pieces. Makes about 1 pound.

The Back Porch Peanut Pie

20 Ritz crackers, finely crushed
¾ cup dry roasted peanuts, crushed medium fine
1 cup sugar
3 egg whites
¼ teaspoon cream of tartar
1 teaspoon vanilla
½ cup sugar
Whipped cream
Shaved bittersweet chocolate

Combine crushed crackers, peanuts and ½ cup sugar; set aside. Make a meringue mixture by beating egg whites with cream of tartar; fold in vanilla until foamy; gradually fold in remaining ½ cup sugar and continue beating until peaks form but mixture is not dry. Fold in cracker mixture. Spread in a greased 9-inch pie pan. Bake in a 325 degree oven for 25 minutes. Cool and refrigerate for three hours. Served topped with whipped cream and sprinkled with shaved bittersweet or unsweetened chocolate. Make one pie.

Peanut Pie

3 eggs
½ cup granulated sugar
1 cup light corn syrup
Pinch of salt
2 tablespoons butter or margarine
3 tablespoons peanut butter
1 teaspoon vanilla
¾ cup roasted peanuts, chopped
1 9-inch unbaked pie shell

Beat eggs and sugar; blend in syrup, salt, butter and peanut butter. Mix thoroughly. Pour into unbaked pie shell. Sprinkle with peanuts.

Bake 400 degrees for about eight minutes or until pastry begins to brown; reduce heat to 300 degrees and continue baking for 35 to 40 minutes or until firm.

Peanutty Apple Upside Down Pie

½ cup chopped salted peanuts
¼ cup light brown sugar, packed
2 tablespoons margarine
1 tablespoon water
1 tablespoon light corn syrup
Pastry for two-crust pie
Peeled, sliced apples to fill pan, about 2½ pounds
⅓ cup sugar
1 tablespoon flour
½ teaspoon ground cinnamon
½ teaspoon nutmeg
1 tablespoon lemon juice

Sprinkle peanuts over bottom of 9-inch pie plate. Set aside.

Combine brown sugar, margarine, water and corn syrup in saucepan. Bring to boil. Cook 3 minutes, stirring. Pour over peanuts.

Prepare pastry. Roll out half of the dough and fit into pie plate. Fill with apple slices.

In a small bowl mix together sugar, flour, cinnamon and nutmeg; sprinkle flour mixture and lemon juice evenly over apples.

Roll out remaining pastry and fit over apple filling. Seal to bottom pastry and flute edge. Cut several slits in top of crust. Bake in hot oven, 400 degrees, about 35 minutes, or until done. Immediately invert onto serving plate; carefully remove pie plate.

Pecan Sandwich Spread

    1 cup pecans
    2 hard-cooked eggs
    1 jar (7 ounces) stuffed olives, drained
    1 medium onion, quartered
    Salt and pepper
    Mayonnaise

Blend pecans, eggs, olives and onion in electric blender. Add salt and pepper to taste and mayonnaise to moisten.

The groves of orchards of pecans trees on all sides of Plains is one of the prettiest of sights. The job of "knocking down," that is, hitting the ripe nuts to make them fall to the ground, was "wimmin's" work.

P.J. Wise recalled that Miss Lillian knocked down pecan trees: "I remember long time ago Mr. Earl had farms and lots of pecan trees and every year he would tell

Miss Lillian that that was her money, to get out and gather the pecans and sell them, and I remember her going to the pecan orchard and knocking down the pecans and gathering them and then taking them to market to make her money . . . yeah, she took 'em herself, knocked them down and everything. That was her responsibility and that was her money. And they've been a progressive family."

Pimento Cheese Spread

1 pound medium to sharp Cheddar cheese
1 can (4 oz.) pimiento cheese
Salt, pepper to taste
A dash of garlic salt
Mayonnaise

Grate cheese. Drain pimiento and reserve liquid. Dice pimiento and add to cheese with salt, pepper, garlic salt and mayonnaise to moisten. If desired, add liquid drained from pimiento to make a softer mixture.

Plains Special Cheese Ring

A Carter family favorite from Rosalynn Carter. Betty Carter (Mrs. Alton) said she brought the recipe for this picture pretty dish to town when she came several years ago.

1 **pound grated cheese**
1 **cup chopped nuts**
1 **cup mayonnaise**
1 **small onion grated**
Black pepper to taste
Dash of cayenne

Mix; mold with hands into desired shape; place in refrigerator until chilled. When ready to serve, fill center
with strawberry preserves. (Good also as cheese spread
without preserves.)

Ambrosia

A Christmas favorite: Ambrosia, which translates as
"food for the gods" is always oranges carefully
peeled and selected and cut into pieces and com-
bined with grated fresh coconut. It may be only
those two ingredients.

6 **large nectarines or peaches or pears peeled, sliced**
3 **large California oranges, peeled, sliced into**
   half cartwheels
1 **large or 2 small bananas, peeled, sliced**
2 **tablespoons sugar**
2 **tablespoons lemon juice**
½ **teaspoon almond extract, optional**
½ **cup flaked coconut**

Combine fruit with sugar, lemon juice and almond extract. Chill for 2 or 3 hours. Spoon into dessert dishes.
Top with coconut. Makes 6 to 8 servings.

Any of these ingredients can be added as desired:
drained crushed pineapple, diced bananas, grapes cut into

halves and seeded. Serve in pretty glass dessert dishes and garnish each serving with a cherry.

Whatever the ingredients, ambrosia is a favorite holiday dessert.

Wines and Southern Hospitality

Southern hospitality was, indeed, in evidence that Saturday afternoon late in August when the gnats were swarming and I dropped in to see Alton Carter, who Maxine Reese said made every kind of wine.

Alton Carter was kneeling in front of the safe in a room in the back of the store he had run for 67 years. His head was in the safe, like the king who was counting his money in a fairy tale. Responding to a question about his winemaking, he said "The best way is to take you and show you how it is done. I can go right now, my house is just up the street, my car is out back, let me get my hat." He got his hat, put it on his head and walked out the back door, leaving the door of the safe wide open.

We got into his car out back of the store. He started up the car; put it in reverse and backed out. His neat white two-story house is on the highway in front of Plains' Main Street. The backyard was filled with the flowers of the kind that have grown in Southern gardens for generations, and on that peaceful Saturday afternoon a hummingbird flitted from blossom to blossom.

The winery is in the building out back. A mere crack in the door makes the nostrils know it is a winery. Alton Carter explains each piece of equipment, mainly wooden kegs, some with their contents bubbling up through glass tubing.

He insisted on drawing out samples for a wine tasting. Tomato wine, pear wine, corn wine. Wow! The corn wine had the kick of a mule and brought to mind a recent wine tasting in Chicago conducted by Michael Broadbent, the suave Englishman who is auctioneer for Christie's in London.

When Broadbent gave a sampling of a collection of '59s, all the biggies, Haut-Brion, Margaux, Petrus, a woman obviously at her first tasting kept asking a group of wine experts, "Tell me what is so great about these wines, just tell me, I want to know."

In Alton Carter's winery, housed in what had once been his smokehouse when he cured meat, there was the same kind of greatness as those '59s, not in his wines, indeed not in his wines, but in him and the warmth of the brand of Southern hospitality he offered as second nature.

How to Make Homemade Wine

From Alton Carter, Jimmy Carter's uncle: "This recipe was used by Father exclusively in 1895 to 1903. He had ten acres in grapes and he made wine of all of them. The law allowed him to sell the wine then but not now. A head of a family is allowed to make as much as 200 gallons by the law, for his own use."

Use either of wood, Greek or glass container (DON'T USE ANYTHING METALLIC). I use a 15 gallon wood keg. This is given for a 15 gallon keg, although you can use any size you like but use quantities according to your container. I make seven different kinds and will try to tell you how each is made.

SCUPPERNONG, TAN AND BLACK, BLACKBERRY

Crush just enough to bust the skin

PEACH

Be sure to peel, not necessary to take out seed or chop.

APPLE, PEAR, TOMATO

Chop up with knife, I cut them in pieces about the size of a normal plum.

Either of the above fruit, put in the wood keg until it is about three-fourths full. Put one gallon of sugar cane syrup (not corn syrup) and pour it into the keg on top of the fruit. Then pour in just enough water to come to the top of the fruit. Let it stand five to ten days. The juice will rot out and go to the bottom and the pulp will come to the top. Draw off the juice (I have a peg in the bottom of my keg). If you don't have a peg, pour out the juice or syphon it out.

I have some five gallon bottles I use. You can use any size bottle you care to or one that is the right size for your amount of juice. I think the most important thing about making wine is getting the correct amount of sugar. Be sure to put in 2½ POUNDS OF SUGAR TO A GALLON. If you don't put in enough it will go to vinegar.

When you get your bottle filled and the right amount of sugar, take the bottle cork, put a hole in the cork and put a small rubber tube in about a foot long. Seal it well without wax, both the rubber tube into the cork and the cork into the bottle. Put the end of the tube into a glass of water. It will work and the gas will bubble out through the water for five to ten weeks according to the cool or hot weather. When it quits bubbling it is ready to be put into a small bottle and used.

When you draw out your first juice, if you care to you can get a second drawing which will be about half as much wine as the first. To do this pour just half as much syrup as you did the first and put enough more water to just cover the fruit. Let it stand another five to ten days. Draw if off and fix it just as you did the first.

Iced Tea By the Gallon

Miss Allie Smith, Rosalynn Carter's mother: "We used to always make my children, we drank milk, until Sunday. We laughed about that. On Sunday I'd give 'em tea," and she laughed again at that memory.

Tea was a boughten thing, milk came from the friendly cow in the backyard.

3 family-sized tea bags
Boiling water
2 cups sugar
2 cups water
2 trays ice

Pour boiling water to cover over tea bags; let steep for exactly five minutes—use timer on stove to be certain. Take out tea bags immediately, pour over sugar. After sugar is dissolved, add two trays of ice and fill gallon container with water.

Punch

1 can (32 or 48 oz.) pink pineapple grapefruit drink
1 can (6 oz.) frozen lemonade concentrate
1 can (No. 2) pineapple juice
1 cup sugar
1 teaspoon almond flavoring
6 bottles (12 oz. each) Fresca
½ gallon (2 quarts) pineapple sherbet

Combine pink pineapple grapefruit drink, undiluted lemonade concentrate, pineapple juice, sugar and almond flavoring; mix and chill.

At serving time, add Fresca and sherbet. Makes about 1½ gallons. Punch is pale pink.

Do not add ice to punch. Make additional mixture of juices; freeze in molds and use as ice.

Punch can be made with plain grapefruit juice instead of pink pineapple grapefruit drink.

If desired, use a 32-ounce can of orange juice instead of grapefruit juice.

A bottle of pink champagne may be added to punch.

—*Angie Stevens*

Lemonade

For a while in the summer of 1976 Amy Carter, daughter of Jimmy and Rosalynn, ran a lemonade stand in Plains, the way children in small towns have enjoyed for generations but hers had to be closed because of too many customers.

6 lemons
1½ cups sugar
2½ quarts water
Ice cubes

Roll lemons with the hands, breaking cells to release juice. Slice one lemon thinly; with a wooden handle pound ½ cup sugar into the sliced lemon. Slice remaining lemons thinly onto first lemon; adding remaining sugar. Let stand for 30 minutes; add water and stir. Add ice cubes. Makes 3 quarts.

VII. The Not-So-Plains Million-Dollar Supper

On October 2, 1976, at Miss Lillian's Pond House in Plains, Ga., the citizens gathered together to hold a $5,000 a plate supper and raised over a million dollars for the Carter presidential campaign. For a glimpse of cooking and socializing, down-South style, have a look at the menu and the particulars of the event:

Menus for the Plains Country Supper

Appetizers Served at the Barbecue Pit

*The Plains Cheese Ring
*Salted Peanuts

A Hoop of Cheddar Cheese

Crackers

Cheese Wafers

Red and Green Pepper Jelly,
Triscuits and Cream Cheese

*Recipes included.

*Fried Chicken
 Barbecued Pig
*Fried Slices of Georgia
   Country Ham
*Butter Beans
 String Beans
 Black-eyed Peas
*Corn Pudding
 Baked Beans
 Beans and Corn
 Whippo'will Peas

Chicken Pies
Roast Turkey with
   Dressing
*Baked Ham
 Succotash
*English Peas
 Turnips with
   Turnip Greens
 Candied Sweet
   Potatoes

Corn-on-the-Cob

*Sweet Potato
   Casserole
*Potato Salad

*Sweet Potato Pudding
*Bean Salad

Congealed Salad

Deviled Eggs

Corn Sticks   *Corn Bread   Mexican Corn Bread

*Yeast Rolls   *Homemade Yeast Bread

Cucumber Pickles *Sweet Pickled Peaches   Beet Pickles

*Pies A Plenty: *Peanut, Pecan, Lemon, German
                  Chocolate

*Great Cakes: White House Cake, *Lane Cake, *Chocolate Cake, Carmel Cake, Mrs. Jimmy Carter's Strawberry Cake, *Coconut Cake, Pecan Cake, Butternut Cake, *Spice Cake

*Banana Puddings

*Iced Tea

*Recipes included.

On that Saturday evening in October, the day after Jimmy Carter's birthday, cooks drove down the red dirt road to Miss Lillian's to bring the specialties each had prepared. The way Maxine Reese talked about planning the supper, she simply asked over 100 volunteers to prepare enough supper, as if they were fixing a Sunday dinner for five persons. "Nobody turned me down," she said. For a gala event, that is a formula simple enough. If 100 persons each cook enough to feed five, there is enough food for 500. Because some of the cooks feared the old Southern stigma of running out of food for their guests, they prepared as much as 50 servings instead of the mere five requested.

When the Peanut Brigade (who had prepared and served the meal) and the guests got to the Pond House, they found Secret Service men all over the place and a table made of planks supported by saw horses placed at an angle just outside the back door. On the table were two of the biggest size tin wash tubs, filled with ice tea. A U-shaped table was in the backyard to hold food. On a slight incline to the right of the table was a barbecue pit, a stone fence, and the tool house, all of which helped to designate the sippin' and snackin' area presided over by the jovial Arthur Cheokas.

The barbecue pit in the upper yard was decorated with clusters of grapes, ears of dried corn, apples, and pumpkins. In addition, there was an arrangement of cattails that prompted a guest to comment, "Those are the biggest corn dogs I ever saw."

In another marked-off area was a trough eight to nine feet long propped up on legs. It was filled with ice and bottles of champagne and chablis and when Arthur Cheokas was asked what it was used for otherwise, said "We buried a fellow in it just last week."

As the cooks arrived with their offerings, attention was caught by the preparation of food committee chairperson

Mrs. Milton Hagerson, who brought a cake on top of which was a miniature White House, a bridegroom figure used to represent Jimmy Carter getting ready for his honeymoon with the country, and a miniature truck filled with peanuts to remind one and all of his down home origins.

From the snacks of Plains' own cheese ring to the barbecued pig the whole presentation was a demonstration, the best ever offered, in Southern cooking.

The main dishes were ham, turkey, and chicken. There were three big trays of thin boneless center slices of fried Georgia country ham. On each platter there was easily the "heart" of three hams; cooks in Plains cherish ham hocks for purposes other than fried ham. The ham had those little white specks in it that baffle ham nonexperts, those same neophytes who think mold on the outside of an uncooked ham indicates spoilage. (The little white specks indicate age on hams saved for special occasions.)

If the quality of the ham at the supper was rated the way a Broadway play is reviewed, the review would say that it was "the best damn ham I've seen in years"—and that in competition with many a finely cured hind leg of a hog. In the language of the area, it was what they call "eatin' high off the hog."

Turkeys roasted to golden succulent goodness were paired with dressing deftly seasoned with garden-grown age. Women in Miss Lillian's kitchen, working as smoothly as helpers in MacDonald's at rush hour, separated the turkey meat from the carcasses, which they piled in a box on the floor. Carved slices of turkey were neatly overlapped on a bed of dressing.

Each piece of the mountains of fried chicken was browned to crisp perfection and as uniform in color as if it had been programmed by a quality control computer. It is difficult to estimate how many pieces of chicken there were on some of the platters. Every Southern cook knows one skillet holds about one chicken. By that token, some of those platters easily held half a dozen chickens.

A topping of marshmallows, both regular and miniature size, on at least a third of the sweet potato casseroles was a significant departure from the past. When marshmallows were first readily available in the 1920's as a store-bought item, a bag cost five cents. They were a luxury compared to foods produced on the place and often appeared only at Thanksgiving and Christmas.

A woman guest asked, "Are there any collards here?" She wanted to be sure if collards were there, that she saw and sampled them.

No, there were no collards. Collards are sometimes served for Sunday dinner, but are most often on the menu for week days. Instead, there was a double-bowl plastic container of turnip greens cooked with diced turnips.

Miss Lillian arrived around 5 p.m. She was every inch the Southern lady immaculate in a white pants suit, white shoes and her white hair neatly coiffed. She had been resting while the others fried the chickens and buttered the beans.

Miss Lillian went from hostess to hostess, each pinned with a peanut as a name tag, saying, "Honey, I am so glad you could come."

Just before the day began to fade into the shadows of twilight, approximately 250 guests from 20 states began to arrive at the Pond House.

The guests came up the path covered with pine needles. They strolled as if at a garden party hosted by Queen Elizabeth at Buckingham Palace. They strolled as slowly as some Southerners talk and their comments of "Why, ah, never saw anything like it in mah life" almost sounded Southern. They spent hours at the Pond House and there was evidence of neither hurry nor boredom.

This was the house that was built by Miss Lillian's children during her sojourn in the Peace Corps in India; it replaced an earlier one that was burned down. It is an angular wooden structure, contemporary, with a driveway that goes up to the back of the house and curves along the side of it.

The front of the house faces the pond, where Miss Lillian often fishes and which is sometimes drained to provide fish for fries. Jimmy Carter has frequently been seen scrambling after fish in the mud after the pond has been drained. The living room of the house is on the pond side and rises two stories with a balcony at the back on the second floor level.

A dozen or more of the guests came in their private planes. They landed on the little air strip in Americus, Ga. Volunteers under the direction of Buford Reese and Dr. David Ewing ran a shuttle-car brigade to pick them up. One out-of-town volunteer at the wheel of a car followed the directions of a volunteer on one trip to the airport. "De airport, it's rite over thah." The airport was right over "thah," in plain sight; but it took half an hour of trial-and-error treks up little roads to reach the strip. Natives know about where the airport is, but they are not accustomed to flying in and out of it.

Leila Barrett, staff writer for the Americus *Times-Recorder*, chatted with Mary Lou Whitney, who came with her husband-philanthropist, Cornelius Vanderbilt Whitney, via a chartered jet from their farm in Lexington, Ky. In Lexington, they are into horses: On the corner of Mrs. Whitney's dark glasses were tiny race horses. The Whitneys brought a pair of the glasses as a gift for Jimmy Carter.

Mrs. Whitney commented on Miss Lillian's Pond House and allowed as how it was smaller than the Whitney's chalet in Switzerland, one of their seven houses around the world (of which two are in Spain).

The conversation turned to Charles A. Lindbergh, who once flew from the field at Americus, the same one where the Whitney jet landed. It seemed that some years ago, according to the Whitneys, "he worked for us" when he was employed by Pan American World Airlines. The Whitneys, of course, have all kinds of Southern and worldwide connections, one being that his brother, Jock, provided some of the financing for *Gone With the Wind*.

Robert Strauss, chairman of the Democratic National Committee, was there with his wife, Helen, who was wearing a full-length dress that looked for all the world like a Crissa. Mrs. Strauss strolled and smiled as she said to ever so many of the volunteer cooks, "You all are so wonderful to do this."

Pat Conner, former treasurer of the committee, was there; and so was the gracious Mrs. Betty Talmadge, wife of Herman, who earlier in the day at their Georgia farm had hosted a Pig Pickin' attended by Mrs. Rosalynn Carter.

Philanthropist Cornelius Vanderbilt Whitney and his wife, Mary Lou, came by chartered jet from their farm in Lexington, Ky. Another Kentuckian there was John J. Brown, former owner of the Kentucky Fried Chicken franchises. John McMillan, from Little Rock, Ark., and Winston Chandler on the Democratic National Finance Committee were also there.

Wallace Hyde, an insurance executive from Asheville, N.C., and fundraiser for the Democratic party for the Southeastern states and coordinator for the supper, was master of ceremonies.

The national press corps was not at the party because the feeling was that for $5,000 a person ought to be entitled to eat dinner without having to answer questions.

Leila Barrett, of the Americus *Times-Recorder*, was there because she is more home folks than press. The Americus *Times-Recorder* for Monday, October 4, 1976, carried this headline on her report on page one: "Event to Remember, 'Plains' Plain Supper' Nets Over $1 Million." She wrote that the event hosted by the Democratic National Committee was dubbed the largest fund-raiser ever staged in Sumter County. Is there another county anywhere that has topped it?

"Then end result of the supper which was attended by over 400 persons, including 222 members of the Democratic party who could afford to pick up the tab on the $5,000-a-plate supper collectively, raised $1.1. . . ." The guests represented 20 states but were basically from 10 Southeastern states.

The Rev. Bruce Edwards of the now-famous First Baptist Church of Plains, Ga., gave the blessing.

During the meal, "Gritz," a blue grass rock band from Furman University, Greenville, S.C., played and sang on a stage bound by bales of straw. A member of the group sang a song—"Peanut Pickin' Politikin' Man"—composed for the occasion. Dr. David Ewing sang "America," had he performed inside, the sound of his opera-quality voice would have "raised the rafters."

The moment came for Jimmy Carter the candidate, who was there with his family, to stand up and speak. He flashed his well-known grin, and although he stood there as a man of destiny, a man in the midst of making history, he came off as a hometown boy home from a week of campaigning.

The crowd chuckled when Jimmy Carter said he wished those "searching for Jimmy Carter could be here now." A ripple of chuckling was followed by a hush of thankfulness and love. It was one of those indescribable moments in life—a time of being caught up in the spirit of man and at the same time a glimpse into something bigger and beyond man: a soul-shaking reminder that the people of the South have been poor and known poverty, but never the poverty of the spirit.

In that moment it was as if a triumphant Confederate Army were marching home singing "Glory, glory, hallelujah! Glory, glory, hallelujah! Glory, glory, hallelujah! His truth is marching on. . . ."

Or as if it were:

A mighty organ with all the stops out playing "Pomp and Circumstance."

The crescendo of Richard Wagner's Ring cycle.

A child's face holding wonder like a cup.

The first crocus of spring.

The message of the earth renewing itself, and the renewal of the spirit of man each Easter.

This was the man Norman Mailer wrote about earlier that same week in the lead article of the New York *Times Magazine* entitled "The Search for Carter": "Happiness came off him. It was as if he knew that God had given him intelligence and good work that would make sense, and so he could give his strength to the world and get new strength back. The emotional meat of the heart might be free of the common bile.

"That helped to explain his smile. Carter smiled because it came easily, and after awhile you hardly noticed it. He had, after all, a lot to smile about; that quiet happiness kept rising out of him. The quiet pleasure of possessing a piece of the cosmos was his; so he kept smiling as naturally as the odor of resin comes off a pine. It was not offensive. It was as if he were offering something you might as well share."[1]

A careful look into the faces of the people seated at the long tables revealed no question, no mysticism about Jimmy Carter as they looked up at him. That man was their "Jimmy" and he was going to be President of the United States.

When there is another edition of the *The American Heritage Cookbook*, an illustrated history of America and drinking with "great traditional recipes and historic menus," let us hope the text will include an account of Miss Lillian's Pond House Supper in the autumn of our bicentennial year. The book gives the menu for Christmas dinner served at Mount Vernon, home of George Washington. It also has the following menu for Lincoln's Inaugural Luncheon: Mock Turtle Soup, Corned Beef and Cabbage, Parsley Potatoes, Blackberry Pie, Coffee. There are menus for meals served at Monticello, home of Thomas Jefferson; for the wedding breakfast of Nellie Grant, the only daughter of President Ulysses Grant; for the Fourth of July Dinner served by John Adams and his wife, Abigail; and the Thanksgiving Dinner from Sagamore Hill, the home of Theodore Roosevelt.

In noting these presidential meals recorded in *The American Heritage* Cookbook, there was no intention to include any of the menus in this book but one: the menu for Christmas Dinner at Mount Vernon, which is included because of the manner in which it compares to the menu for the Plains country supper:

Christmas Dinner at Mount Vernon

An Onion Soup Call'd the King's Soup

Oysters on the Half Shell   Broiled Salt Roe
Boiled Rockfish   Herring
Roast Beef and Yorkshire Pudding   Mutton Chops
Roast Sucklin Pig   Roast Turkey with Chestnut Stuffing
Round of Cold Boiled Beef   Cold Baked Virginia
      with Horseradish Sauce   Ham—
Lima Beans   Baked Acorn Squash   Baked Celery with
                                                      Slivered Almonds
Hominy Pudding   Candied Sweet Potatoes
Cantaloupe Pickle   Spiced Peaches in Brandy
Spiced Cranberries   Mincemeat Pie   Apple Pie
Cherry Pie   Chess Tarts   Blancmange
Plums in Wine Jelly   Snowballs   Indian Pudding
      Great Cake   Ice Cream   Plum Pudding
            Fruits   Nuts   Raisins
                  Port Madeira

VIII. Election Night in Plains

The red telephone on the wall in the kitchen of Sybil and Billy Carter's home was dangling by the cord when a crowd arrived sometime before midnight the night of the election, Tuesday, November 2, 1976. The phone was still dangling Wednesday morning at 10:45 a.m., the morning the outcome was a certainty.

If the telephone had rung during that long night, there was so much noise in the house that the ring probably would not have been heard. No one thought of going to bed all night, not until after the daylight celebration at the train station. When Billy Carter returned to his living room after dawn, he put his head down on a pillow that faced the three television sets, one on NBC, one on ABC and one on CBS. They had been on all night and were still on at 10:45 a.m., when Billy Carter finally went to sleep. By then, there were seven others sound asleep in the Carter living room.

Sybil, Billy Carter's wife, was still up. She had not slept a wink all night and when asked how she did it, she answered, "People born and raised on a farm don't stop." "If you are married to a Carter, you just do it. Billy 'volunteers' me, Jimmy 'volunteers' me. They say, 'Sybil, she'll do it' and I do, you just do."

The evening started at suppertime when there was a community barbecue served under tents in the center of town. Men barbecued halves of chickens and served them with coleslaw and hush puppies.

Everybody knew it would be a long night and was filled with apprehension, and downright fear. The political polls at the time of the Democratic National Convention showed Jimmy Carter with an almost unbeatable lead over President Gerald Ford, but by the eve of the election most of the pollsters said the race was too close to call and the people of Plains knew they were in for a cliff-hanger.

Jimmy Carter and Rosalynn had gotten up early that day and voted in Plains, where the Press spent the day until after Carter spoke at 5 p.m. at the train station, one last short speech before going to Atlanta for the long wait.

At about 7 p.m. at the airport in Albany, Ga., a porter announced, "Here dey come!" The entourage of motorcycles, police cars with flashing blue lights, long sleek black Cadillacs, and two buses wheeled in. Secret Service men lined the field inside the fence over which a few people leaned.

The news media got out of the buses, and those carrying heavy television cameras walked like infantry soldiers after a long battle. Their feet moved as if leaden. Not so with Jimmy Carter. He jumped out of the car and was smiling and waving as he went up the steps of his aircraft, Peanut One. He was carrying his own blue garment bag and Mrs. Carter was carrying her own bag, as was their custom throughout the campaign.

After the barbecue supper in the square, about two thousand people were milling around Main Street, the train station and in the Back Porch Cafe, which had posted a sign, "We Do Not Have a Public Restroom." A couple of portable toilets were down the street.

At the home of a friend of Jimmy Carter, Nub Chappell, a crowd had gathered. Chappell had said, "Come over to my place," and he had plenty of refreshments, a ham and snacks in the kitchen.

Guests milled in and out of the living room where three television sets reported fragmented returns. The talk was more about trivia than anything else. No one mentioned the possibility that Jimmy Carter would lose the election, but that chilling thought was there the same way a chill fills the hearts of those waiting outside the door of a beloved and critically ill patient in a hospital room. There was basis for hope and it flickered in and out of the heart like the flame of the matches lit in the story about "The Little Match Girl" who was out in the cold and had only a box of matches to keep her from freezing on a cold night.

When Walter Cronkite mentioned Robert Strauss, chairman of the Democratic National Party, and called him Rodgers, everybody laughed louder than that slip of the tongue warranted, the way tense people laugh at anything the least bit funny to break the monotony.

The crowd reminisced about the time Jimmy did this or that or something his Daddy, Mother, Gloria or Ruth did—the way people talk in a small town at a family reunion, wedding or funeral.

Early in the evening, we said to Mrs. Laura Dudley of Richland, Ga., that we had come there as strangers and "we felt like one of them."

Mrs. Dudley hit the ceiling, meaning she acted like she was mad as a wet hen at the mention of the word "stranger." "You're no stranger, you are my friend," she said, and you knew you were. She issued a firm invitation to come for a visit to the boat "we have tied up in the Gulf. We can't sleep but about six or eight but there's a motel across the way where you can stay and we can go out on the boat and fish and have picnics and so much fun," she said, and you knew she meant that, too.

Every once in a while Nub Chappell answered the

phone and came back to say that Billy had called and said, "Come on over to my place." Billy, the brother of Jimmy Carter.

In Southern towns where there is characteristically nothing to do but "get together," a favorite activity for a crowd is to go from house to house. Deciding who will ride with whom, loading the cars, having a flat tire, drinking out of a "Coke-coler" bottle with peanuts down in it, giving out of gas and having to push the car, just getting there—these are all part of making an evening interesting.

After Billy Carter called once again, Nub Chappell said, "Guess we better go on over to Billy's." Then began the talk about which cars to take, which to leave, who would ride in each car. When the caravan reached Billy's home, it was like a family reunion: There was kissin' and huggin' and invitations to "come on in the house"—all serving to break the monotony of waiting and the lonely chill that went with it.

It was 11 o'clock.

The three television sets in Billy Carter's living room were going full blast and the room was filled with people sitting around in chairs, on arms of chairs, on stools, on the floor, as if at a boxing match or in a small theater. Billy was on the floor to the left of the television sets.

Suddenly, at 11:20 p.m. someone says, "If we just get New York! When New York comes in, we've got it!"

Billy Carter yelled "Come on, New York!" the way a man roots for his favorite football player running toward a touchdown. The people of Plains were used to having a winning team. Carlton Walton, coach of the basketball team at Plains High School, said in his eight years as coach the team won 188 games and lost 44.

At first New York did not "come in" for Carter and later, after it had been predicted for Carter, an announcement was made that someone, perhaps from the White House, was going to impound the 25,000 voting machines in the state of New York and hold them until a recount could be made. A gut groan went out over Billy Carter's living room. It was as if their favorite football player had one foot in the end zone without one tackler in sight and a flag was thrown on the play. Would New York be called back?

Someone said, "If Illinois would just come in, there will be enough votes from Cook County. Ohio is good, we're going well in the rural areas. . . ."

12:45 a.m.: "Now as soon as we get Hawaii, we've got 271. Hawaii will be no problem, everybody knows it is Carter country." But Hawaii didn't come in either.

1:10 a.m. One set shows the Ohio results with Ford and Carter neck and neck. Then they show Democrat Howard Metzenbaum pulling ahead of his rival in the Ohio Senate race. That seemed like a good sign when a straw in the flood would have seemed like a floating tree. "Right on, Metzenbaum!"

Another television set shows Carter with 51, Ford 48 with 69 percent of the returns in.

1:20 a.m. "It looks like we've lost Hawaii. It's serious."

There was the challenge to the results in New York and the battles in California, Oregon, and Ohio were neck-and-neck. Even Mississippi, which was showing Carter 51, Ford 48, with 85 percent of the vote counted, was not considered sure enough to bring cheers.

"It ain't just nail-biting time, I'm ready to start chewing fingers," one man said.

Said another: "It's there, it's gonna happen for us, we'll take one more state somewhere for sure. I wish it would happen soon. I'd like to get it over."

It did not happen and the people were going in and out of the living room and kitchen, where there was a bounty of food and drink, and in and out of the bathrooms like ants in and out of an ant hill.

2 a.m. It had not yet happened. Two and a half hours after it should have seemed certain, it had not happened.

More waiting.

It was a moment like waiting for "the dawn's early light," or the passing of a fever; it was a time of knuckle-biting, hand-wringing and walking the floor.

During those hours in the middle of the night in Billy Carter's living room, there wasn't much humor. The crowd was weary to the head-nodding stage and ached when an announcer said that the outcome of the election may not be known for days after a count of absentee ballots. It was a time for survival fellowship.

3:28 a.m. CBS declared that Hawaii was Carter's and the weary, bleary-eyed watchers scrambled to their feet.

Billy Carter pulled off his shirt to reveal a bright green T-shirt with white letters that said:

Jimmy Won!
'76

And about that time on the television set was Miss Lillian wearing the same green T-shirt, beaming and grinning the Carter grin.

And then, three minutes later, NBC flashed a sign on the screen: "Carter Elected" and the Carter house rocked on its foundations with an alive, wide-awake crowd jumpin' up and down cheerin' and yellin' their heads off and huggin' and cryin' and kissin'.

Billy Carter kept referring to the polls with words not fittin' for ears of a lady and the polls said "didn't more'n one or two per cent of the people even knew who Jimmy Carter was a year ago."

Some of the crowd climbed into cars while others walked like soldiers fresh from victory to the town square. In minutes a crowd had gathered at the train station. Everyone who could grab one of the green Jimmy Won T-shirts selling for $4 got one and put it on. None of it seemed real. It was still dark and the train station, this time for sure like a set for a movie, was lighted brighter than day from the battery of spotlights on the buildings across the street.

Members of the "peanut brigade" campaign workers, nurtured throughout the long campaign by high priestess Maxine Reese, were there. And Maxine's husband, Buford, was there on the train station platform. Maxine Reese said she wishes she had kept a diary beginning when she and other members of the peanut brigade went to New Hampshire in the dead of winter when "Ah nearly froze to death" and began ringing doorbells. When someone came to the door, Maxine Reese and others said, "I would like for you to vote for Jimmy Carter." The now-famous answer often was "Jimmy who?"

Since Maxine Reese's triumphant return from the Democratic National Convention in New York City when Jimmy Carter was nominated, she had unswervingly referred to him as "President Carter"; for in her mind and heart he was. Her fervor was an inspiration, merely by the fact one person in the world had that depth of belief. And now it was a fact that Maxine Reese's President Carter was to be everybody's President Carter. And now she could say to the train conductor, "Bring the train on in January. We're going to load it to go to Washington for the Inauguration." In the summer of 1976 Maxine Reese had rented a train for that purpose.

Dr. David Ewing, dressed in a pale blue suit, got at the podium and belted out "America." He followed with "Amazing Grace," Jimmy Carter's favorite hymn, and continued with "Dixie."

It was a moment of victory that topped the one when Jimmy Carter spoke at the Million Dollar Supper, for this time enough votes were in to put him in the White House. Maxine and Buford Reese, and June and David Ewing, and all the other hard workers had won. They knew all along in their hearts that it was right for Jimmy Carter to win, because he was a winner, that the future of this country was safe in his hands; but the past few weeks had put fear in their hearts, fear that a society dominated by polls and computers rather than independent thinking might not cast enough votes. The victory scene at dawn was straight out of a movie. A Danish newsman kept saying, "Only in America could it happen."

The crowd milled and thinned out a little as it waited for Jimmy Carter to return from Atlanta, where he had watched the returns. There he was that Wednesday morning once more up on the platform at the train station just as he had been after each primary. This time after an all-night vigil, victory was his. Carter said the first task must be "the unification of our country after a close and hard-fought election."

The poignancy of the welcome by those who had not only stayed up through the night but had supported his candidacy all those months engulfed Jimmy Carter. "I came all the way through 22 months, and I didn't get choked up until I . . ." His voice trailed off, and he embraced his wife, Rosalynn, who wept with him.

IX. Carter Country Tour

Every visitor to Plains wants to see the background from which Jimmy Carter came. Before Carter, visitors might have driven through without noticing the town. Now they have not only seen it on television and in all types of pictures, but they have a chance of reading about Plains in a way that hopefully brings them closer to its citizens. Still, it isn't the same as being there, as talking with one of the natives direct; and so, in this chapter, we present Dr. David Ewing and his tour of Plains.

A brief word on Dr. Ewing: A baritone, who loves to sing "How Great Thou Art" at the Plains Baptist Church, he has an Ed. D. from the University of Georgia, with special emphasis on math and physics. The tour originated in the spring when he was talking to visitors at the Carter campaign headquarters in Plains. As more and more visitors arrived—and as it got harder for the townspeople to conduct their daily business without being pestered—he received permission to conduct an insider's tour of the outside of Plains. This he does in his own inimitable manner from one of two Dodge maxi-wagons.

Plains may appear to be merely a row of stores—the Peanut Patch, a shop with mostly peanut things; the Peanut Museum; the Back Porch Cafe; Turner's Hardware and Department Store, the Carter Worm Farm Office (Billy Carter runs what is reportedly the largest worm farm in the world); Sand Crafts; Walters' Grocery; Carter Antiques and Country Store; and others.

Perhaps a visitor might also run into the type of problem encountered by reporter James T. Wooten of the New York *Times:* "Visibility has always been a problem in Southern villages. There is just so much an outsider is allowed to see; although what is concealed is generally done so cordially, hidden by soft drawls, enigmatic smiles and invitations to come back again soon.

" 'I believe a fellow could stay here a year or more and ask all the right questions and never get all the right answers.' " Hugh Carter, the 55-year-old cousin of the President-elect, philosophized recently.

"Is that xenophobic?

" 'Nope, that's just how it is.'

"Why is it that way?

" 'Because some things are nobody's business.'

"What things?"

" 'That's nobody's business.'

"Do people in Plains have something to hide?

" 'I expect so,' said Mr. Carter. 'Doesn't everybody?' "[1]

Climb aboard Dr. Ewing's small bus and listen to him give his tour his way, with his style, and gain another insight into the South:

Welcome to Plains, Georgia, home of the President of the United States! The religious influence on this region dates back to its inception. Plains was named for the Plain of Dura. King Nebuchadnezzar built a golden idol ninety feet tall upon the Plain of Dura. When Plains moved two miles to be closer to the railroad track, they shortened the name to "The Plains." The Carter family came to Plains in 1830, just after the Indians moved out. Our first point of interest will be the home of the mayor of Plains, Mr. A. L. Blanton. Mr. Blanton is the air traffic controller at the Albany airport. It's the house with the green roof, white with black trim.

Mrs. Lillian Carter, Jimmy's mother, sold that home to Mr. Blanton. The church that you see coming into view is the Plains Baptist Church, a pretty, white church. Among the many people who worship there are Jimmy, Rosalynn, Amy, Miss Lillian, and a lot of members of the Carter family and the community. Beside the church is the home of the pastor. It's traditional for the congregation to own not only the sanctuary but also the home of the pastor.

Jimmy returned to Plains in 1953 when his father died. He came home to take over the family business. As he returned home he and Rosalynn dropped by the office of their congressman, Tic Forrester. Mr. Forrester gave them the standard tour of the capital, and in so doing he told them about the living conditions in public housing. Jimmy and Rosalynn just looked at each other and didn't say a word, because they were moving into the public housing up here on the left. It's in this first unit, and it's in the apartment on the right hand side just under the mimosa tree. When Jimmy comes home today there are usually hundreds of people waiting on him and it's quite an event. Sometimes he likes to recall that it was not such a momentous occasion when he returned to Plains in 1953. Now if you look over on the right, you'll see a field of peanuts. Those are Jimmy Carter's peanuts. Now the peanuts are the roots of those plants out there.

Our next point of interest will be Jimmy's first public service project. When Jimmy returned to Plains and the hot weather came around, he said what Plains, Georgia, needs is a swimming pool. And this is the fruition of his effort. He presented this idea to the Lions' Club and got them mobilized behind him. This served as a great encouragement to a young Jimmy Carter, showing him that one concerned and energetic man could make a difference. The greyish green building is the building of the Lions' Club.

Now we'll catch a glimpse of Jimmy's house from the other end of the barricaded street.

Jimmy went on to become district governor of the Lions' Club. He made friends throughout the state. He got to see the wonderful work that a civic organization can do and the way of humanitarian endeavors. But he was also impressed with the limitations that you have with a volunteer group, and this led him into politics. He began to believe that perhaps a dedicated and concerned public official could make a greater impact, and he ran for the state senate and eventually for governor of the state of Georgia.

Ahead of us now is a red brick building, and that's the Plains High School, from which Jimmy graduated at the head of his class in 1941. He went from there to the local college, Georgia Southwestern, where he spent a year. From there he went to Georgia Tech, and then to the Naval Academy.

When he got to the Naval Academy at Annapolis, some of his acquaintances were a bit skeptical of his ability, since he had come from a small farming community in Georgia. Jimmy says that Annapolis was tough, but Georgia Tech was just a little bit tougher.

Now back to the left is the Plains Baptist Church, a very picturesque building and perhaps a little larger than you had anticipated. Over on the right is the Lutheran Church. The grey house following the Lutheran Church is the home of the pastor of that church.

Our next point of interest will be the home of Jimmy's younger brother by some thirteen years, Billy Carter. It's the grey house on the left with a basketball goal in the yard. Billy lives there with his wife Sybil and five children. They have another child on the way.

Ahead is one of the many fine convalescent facilities here in this region. . . . It used to be a hospital and was operated by a family of doctors by the name of Wise. Miss Lillian received her training as a registered nurse there. I'll go slowly so that you can look through the columns on the left-hand side of the building and see the smallest window. The next window after that is the room where Miss Lillian gave birth to her first child, James Earl Carter, Jr., known affectionately as Jimmy. I expect sometime soon there'll be a marker there to indicate the place of Jimmy's birth. Can you see the marker in front of the window now? It says "No Parking."

And if you were to take a left at the next intersection and go down about 2 miles, you'd come to the Plains Agricultural Experiment Station, where research is done on hybrid seeds and fertilizers to determine the products that grow best in this part of the country.

But we're going to take a right, and you'll see what appears to be an ordinary water tank. But look closely; appearances can be deceiving. Up on the catwalk you'll see the dish of a microwave antenna used to relay messages from local television facilities to national headquarters. At the base of the tank, you'll see three mobile homes for ABC, CBS, and NBC. That's Television City, downtown Plains, Georgia.

Now off to the right, behind the metal building, is the softball field where Jimmy plays ball with the newsmen. Newsmen will sometimes ask loaded questions, but so far the only time they've gotten Jimmy to play ball with them is when he's out there on the playing field.

The buildings on the left house facilities for processing local agricultural products, such as cotton and peanuts. In the distance is a large yellow warehouse. That's on Carter property. All the buildings on the other side of the railroad tracks belong to the Carter family. Many men have gotten into politics to make money. Jimmy has made money so he can get into politics without selling out to some special interest group.

Now we have a Plains exclusive: It's the Plains, Ga., Men's Club. You may not recognize it right away because it's disguised as a service station. The proprietor is Billy Carter, Jimmy's younger brother. They have a standing agreement at the station that if someone's wife calls, he just left.

Over on the left now, we have a state park located in downtown Plains with shade trees, picnic tables, and don't forget the trash cans.

Also on the left is the home of Jimmy's mother, Miss Lillian. It's the modest brick home.

The red brick church coming up is the Methodist Church of Plains. Behind the church is a white house, that's where Jimmy's aunt lived while he was growing up. He and his sister Gloria had their meals with the aunt and

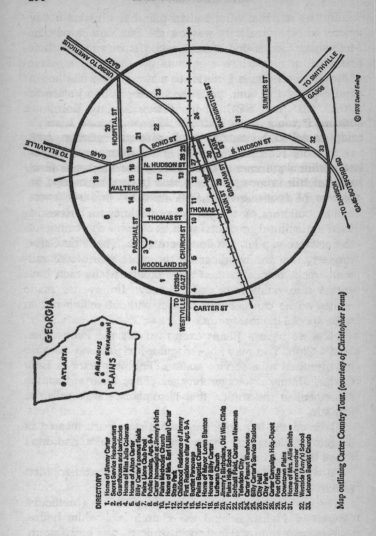

GEORGIA

ATLANTA

AMERICUS
PLAINS • SAVANNAH

DIRECTORY

1. Home of Jimmy Carter
2. Secret Service Headquarters
3. Guardhouses and barricades
4. Home of Miss Julia Coleman
5. Home of Alton Carter
6. Billy Carter's peanut fields
7. Plains Lions Club Pool
8. Public Library, Apt. 9-A
9. Carter homesight at Jimmy's birth
10. Plains Methodist Church
11. Home of Mrs. Earl (Lillian) Carter
12. State Park
13. Childhood Residence of Jimmy
14. First Residence after Apt. 9-A
15. Baptist Church
16. Plains Baptist Church
17. Home of Mayor Loren Blanton
18. Lutheran Church
19. Home of Billy Carter
20. Jimmy's Birthplace, Old Wise Clinic
21. Plains High School
22. Softball Field, Carter vs Newsmen
23. Television City
24. Carter Peanut Warehouse
25. Billy Carter's Service Station
26. City Hall
27. City Park
28. Carter Campaign Hdq.-Depot
29. Post Office Plains
30. Downtown Plains
31. Home of Mrs. Allie Smith —
   Rosalynn's mother
32. Westside (Amy's) School
33. Lebanon Baptist Church

Map outlining Carter Country Tour, *(courtesy of Christopher Fenn)*

© 1976 David Ewing

Jimmy tells me that Miss Lillian paid her a nickel a day apiece for the meals. It was on the front steps of that Methodist Church that Jimmy asked Rosalynn for their first date.

Now over on the left you'll see a two-story white house coming into view, and that's the home of Jimmy's Uncle Alton. He's usually working down at the Antique Store.

Now, if you will, look off to the right: there's Jimmy's and Rosalynn's house. On this end of the building you'll see the roof reflecting the light, and some green siding—that's Jimmy's library. There's the rest of the house now, with brick and mortar, windows and some columns. In the front of the house is Amy's lemonade stand which was abandoned when the road was blockaded. There's a guardhouse. See the plainclothesman! He's a member of the Secret Service. It will become increasingly difficult for Amy and her father to keep in touch with the common people. But it has to be that way for security reasons, and we certainly understand.

Jimmy has added a library to his house. He has hundreds upon hundreds of books. All of his adult life he's read several books a week. He read *War and Peace* at the age of 12.

As we come to the city limits of Plains we see peanut fields right up to the city limits. You might have expected that. And the pecan trees off in the distance are used as a source of supplementary income. You can see pecan trees around a person's house up here. They're gathered in the late fall. Some people even use pecans to pay their taxes. Drives the goverment nuts!

Beneath those pecan trees coming into view is a place for a vegetable stand when vegetables are in season. Next is a field of cotton. And off in the distance, you might recognize a field of corn. All of these agricultural products just about give you Georgia's agricultural productivity in a nutshell, maybe a peanut shell. Cotton was king for a number of years. Georgia is known as the Peach State. If you go down the road about 40 miles east of here, you'll come to Cordele, Georgia, which they call the watermelon capital of the world. Americus and Albany vie for being the pecan capital while Plains and Dawson vie for being the peanut capital.

Now coming up on the left we're going to see the haunted house that Jimmy and Rosalynn lived in after they moved out of public housing. Now the mobile home there, the other house. I've never heard of a haunted mobile home, have you?

Our next point of interest will be the Lebanon Cemetery, the final resting place of many of the Plains inhabitants. It used to be said that there were a lot more people lying down than there were walking around. With the worldwide population explosion, that is no longer the case. And with problems like the population explosion, pollution, depletion of our natural resources and the energy crisis, we need a man of great wisdom, compassion, but most of all judgement, in a position of leadership. Now I'm not chauvinistic about it. I know Jimmy Carter to be just as human as the next person. But Jimmy will do his best, and his best is just about the best than can be done.

Over on the right we have the beginning of the old Carter farm, where Jimmy Carter grew up. It's no longer Carter property. But if you would, imagine in your mind's eye a little freckle-faced, towheaded, barefoot boy scampering through the fields, swinging in the trees, and doing some chores, then you've got yourself a picture of Jimmy Carter some 40 to 45 years ago. The green house is where an American Indian lived while Jimmy was growing up. And the barn following that is the barn where Jimmy did many of his chores. Miss Lillian does not remember Jimmy doing as many chores as Jimmy does . . . but that's a mother for you.

Off in the distance now you'll see a red building coming into view, and that was the family store, called a commissary. Jimmy took his turn along with Gloria and Ruth, minding the store. They sold cured ham and other products of their labor, such as their own brand of Plains-made syrup.

Between the store and the house was a tennis court. Jimmy's father, Mr. Earl, loved to play tennis and he could beat Jimmy playing tennis even after Jimmy grew up. Wealthy people can't imagine there being a tennis court without a tennis pro and a club house, but you can see that all we needed in the south as a flat piece of dirt.

And now we have the boyhood home of Jimmy Carter, which was painted white while he was growing up. Here beside the road we see an old pecan tree with a limb sawed off. We know it's old because that's where Jimmy had his favorite tree house. One night Mr. Earl was having party for some friends and it got so boisterous that Jimmy couldn't go to sleep. So Jimmy went outside, crawled up in his tree house, curled up and went to sleep. Presently Miss Lillian came home from a nursing assignment: "Where's Jimmy?" They searched for Jimmy high and low and couldn't find him anywhere. He heard their calls, but he wouldn't come down. When finally he did come down, Mr. Earl was waiting for him with a switch, a peach tree switch. Now that's the worst kind. Jimmy says he got one of the six switches that he ever got in his life. He remembers all six of them. He doesn't hold a grudge you understand, he's just got a good memory.

Off to the left here you'll see some large pecan trees. When Jimmy was just a slip of a lad he helped his father plant those pecan trees. Today he sees those trees and how big they've grown, and he can't believe that he's as old as those pecan trees; but I'm afraid he is.

Off to the right you'll see a railroad track that has gone by the house for a long, long time. Now railroad tracks have had an effect on a number of people who have lived by them. And I don't know but what that particular railroad track has had an effect on Jimmy. You can picture a little boy tossing in his bed at night, listening to that train off in the distance. I'm sure it made him think about places far away, and wonder what sort of people were there. Jimmy has a compassion for all people, and he really enjoys meeting them. Politicians who don't enjoy meeting people have to put up a front all the time and are under a tension. That's one of the secrets of Jimmy's tirelessness. The friendly person you see is just Jimmy Carter being himself. (Miss Lillian told me that another secret of her tirelessness and Jimmy's is the food they eat. They eat peanuts.)

... Now, I said this used to be a dirt road and I wouldn't want you to experience a dirt road vicariously, so I'm going to take you on one right now. If you were at Disney World you'd pay your price of admission just to ride on a road like this. And they would call it a roller coaster. But there's no extra charge for this. You're going to have to hold on.

We have a field that's devoted to peanuts on the right and a cotton field on the left. Some time ago we had one of those pseudo-intellectuals that you've heard about come into Plains. She approached me and said, "I didn't come here to take any tour. I didn't come here to see Jimmy or his house or anything else. I'm a people watcher. I came here to see all these crazy people coming from all over the world. I can't understand them. What brings them here? There's nothing in Plains." And I said, "Ma'am, have you ever been to Disney World?" And she said, "That's absurd. That's a lot of fun, but it's phony and plastic and artificial. It's just the opposite of this." And I said, "That's exactly my point. This is the antithesis of anything phony. This is where an outstanding leader was born and this is where he was raised. These are the surroundings that produced a Jimmy Carter. It's seldom that we get a chance to have history in the making. No, this isn't phony, this is the real thing."

Now over on the right you have a field of peanuts. You may be a dyed-in-the-wool city slicker from downtown Albany, Georgia, but you can't look at that field of peanuts and tell me it's not a thing of beauty. Albany's about as cosmopolitan as I can get.

Over on the right now, with the stand of pine trees there, we have the beginning of Miss Lillian's property. Those pine trees are all about the same size. They don't grow that way in nature. On the lefthand side, you'll see how nature grows pine trees, all random sizes. Those pine trees on the right that belong to Miss Lillian were planted under a government soil bank program. Farmers were paid to take their acreage out of cultivation and plant it in pine trees. They're a little too big now. The smaller ones should be thinned out to be used for pulp wood and the larger ones left to grow into saw timber. But I understand that the Carters have something on their minds lately besides peanuts and pine trees.

Now Miss Lillian and Amy used to come out here quite a bit, and we're coming to the place where they stayed, the Pond House. Miss Lillian said she came out here to get away from the hectic life of downtown Plains, Georgia. And if you look off to the right there, you'll see the Pond House. And to the left of the house, you'll see a hammock hanging between two trees. That hammock belongs to Miss Lillian. Her grandson Jack made it for her. Mabye you've heard of Jack's mother and daddy, Rosalynn and Jimmy. They're just regular folks.

Over to the right behind the bushes is the pond. Not long ago Jimmy had a fish-fry at that pond. It was on the occasion of his return from the primaries. When he got back from the primaries, he looked at the Secret Service men and they were exhausted. He looked at the newsmen and they were devastated. And he said: "I'm going to have a party for you fellows," and some of them just muttered and groaned and said, "Oh, no, I'd just rather rest." But he went ahead and got together some of his local friends and drained the pond in preparation for the fishfry. Jimmy went down into the mud and water with a net and up he came with a big fish struggling in the net and mud dripping from every fiber. When Sam Donaldson of ABC saw him, he said, "Any man that'll get down in the mud like that can't be all bad." Sam's learning. . . .

Now Jimmy's had an idea about judging people for a long time. As he tells it, when he was a little boy he used to walk barefoot along the railroad tracks back there into Plains to sell little bags of boiled peanuts. Says he learned to tell the good guys from the bad guys. The good guys bought his peanuts. Now that was when he was seven years old. He's grown a lot since then, and he's got other ways of telling the good guys from the bad guys today.

If you were to continue on down this road about three more miles, you'd come to a major part of Jimmy's farmland. It lies in Webster County. Jimmy has between three and four thousand acres in all. Some of the property that's in the Carter family today has been in the family for five generations. Farms today are not necessarily operated by the landowner. The landowner may lease property to the farmer and the two of them will share the profits.

On the side of the road you'll see some large vines. Those vines are kudzu, k-u-d-z-u, and we're going to see more and more of it. A fellow Georgian brought that kudzu into this country some years ago as an experiment to hold back soil erosion. Brought it in from Japan—going to do better than nature. Nine times out of ten when we try to outdo nature we make a mess of it. Nature's been in the process of research and development of this delicate plant for over three billion years. Man in his conceit thinks that he has infinite wisdom. He blunders along and makes a mess like you see up here on the side of the road. The kudzu draping over the trees cuts off photosynthesis, and the trees die. Kudzu is destructive and detestable.

Behind this house on the left you'll see a swimming pool where Rosalynn and Jimmy and Amy often take a dip. That's the property of Jimmy's first cousin, State Senator Hugh Carter. You'll also see a road that goes down to the left, a dirt road. It goes behind Hugh's house and to the world's largest worm farm. Hugh has made a worm farm into a lucrative business. He sells worms all over the world from monthly advertisements in *Outdoor Life* and *Sports Afield*.

Over on the right you'll see a pond—a pretty little pond. Ponds serve several functions in this region. They're a source of water for the animals, irrigation for the crops, recreation, but most of all they supply one of the three basic necessities of life, food. If you have a good catfish pond you could raise more pounds of food per acre than if you devoted the same acreage to the raising of beef cattle.

Over behind this grove of pecan trees on the right is a huge field, 800 acres of it. We'll see more of that field as we round the curve up here. That field used to be used as a practice landing field by the Air Force during World War II. All that's left of its former glory is just a small private landing strip for private planes and crop dusters. When Jimmy was running for governor, Hugh across the road could hear him taking off every morning before dawn and going all over the state of Georgia in his private plane. When Fritz Mondale received the vice-presidential nomination, he was criticized for not being an avid campaigner. Fritz said, "I'm going to get up an hour before Jimmy Carter. I'm going to go to bed an hour after Jimmy Carter." Hamilton Jordan, Jimmy's campaign manager, was asked about Mondale's statement. Hamilton said, "It'll kill him." It's hard to keep up with Jimmy Carter.

The property we're passing through right now belongs to Jimmy's sister Gloria Spann. Gloria is noted for riding a motorcycle, but she is more than a motorcyclist. She's been an accomplished artist all her adult life. Jimmy's other sister, Ruth Stapleton, is an evangelist, and she lives in Fayetteville, North Carolina. . . .

Off to the right is the elementary school where Amy went to the second and third grade. She starts fourth grade there this fall. I understand that she'll be changing schools in January. That lovely family is planning to move out of the community, but we understand that they're desperately needed elsewhere in the country, and her father will be taking an important job with the government.

Now straight ahead of us we see a light grey home. That's where Rosalynn grew up. Her mother, Mrs. Alice Smith, still lives there. Mrs. Smith recently retired from the postal service. Rosalynn's father died when Rosalynn was thirteen and she's been working ever since. All the Carter women are doers. Rosalynn would be miserable if she had to just sit on a cushion all the time and meet dignitaries as First Lady. She'll be a working First Lady. One of her pet projects is mental health. She'll be working on that project and many others. Rosalynn is Jimmy's chief adviser, and I think she's probably his best adviser.

Now coming up we're going to have a little rendezvous with extra sensory perception. We have a street up here that's on Carter Warehouse property. Notice the name of the street—a little precognition—the name is Washington Street. Jimmy's been on the road to Washington longer than most of us realize. In all fairness, though, it was George Washington Carver who introduced the peanut as a major crop in the South. He found over 200 uses for it.

Now if you were to go down Washington Street you'd

come to a brand-new peanut sheller that cost over a million dollars. It uses an electric eye to separate the good peanuts from the bad, and it's got enough sense to just shell the good ones. I wish I knew enough to separate the good guys from the bad guys. Most of the time I can't tell the difference, but I think I'm on to something! The good guys take my tour.

And so, welcome to Main Street, Plains, Georgia, U.S.A. I want you to notice the balance of stores and services here in Plains—and it was before the days of shopping centers that Plains was built. We have the Peanut Patch Novelties; a museum coming in; Carter-Mondale press office; the Back Porch Cafe; Turner Hardware and Department Store; Sandcraft Handmade Novelties; upstairs over the grocery store Carter Antiques; a bank; another grocery store; a drug store; a post office; across the tracks over there is a coin shop and a presidential headquarters. Many times people have talked to me about progress coming to Plains. I suggest that others might come to Plains to see what progress is all about. Jimmy Carter came from Plains just about like you see it right now, and if it's good enough to produce a Jimmy Carter, it just might be all right.

I appreciate you folks coming to Plains.

Notes

I. Miss Lillian

1. Peter Goldman and Eleanor Clift, "Carter on the Rise," *Newsweek*, 8 March 1976, p. 24, quoted in *Jimmy Who?* by Leslie Wheeler (Woodbury, N.Y.: Barron's Educational Series, Inc., 1976), p. 156.

2. "The Whole Carter Family Joins Scramble for White House," *U.S. News & World Report*, 26 July 1976, p. 27.

3. Claire Safran, "The Women in Jimmy Carter's Life," *Redbook*, October 1976, p. 82.

4. Nanette Rainone, Mary King, and Peter Bourne, interviewers, "Lillian Carter Talks about Racism, the Kennedys, and 'Jimmy's Reign,' " *Ms.*, October 1976, p. 88.

5. Ibid., p. 86.

6. "Carter Up Close: 'He Never Gives Up,' " *Newsweek*, 19 July 1976, p. 20.

7. Howard Norton and Bob Slosser, *The Miracle of Jimmy Carter* (Plainfield, N.J.: Logos International, 1976), pp. 22-23.

8. Bill Schemmel, "My Son Jimmy," *Ladies Home Journal*, August 1976, p. 73.

II. Miss Lillian, Matriarch

1. Nanette Rainone, Mary King, and Peter Bourne, interviewers, "Lillian Carter Talks About Racism, the Kennedys, and 'Jimmy's Reign,' " *Ms.*, October 1976, p. 51.

2. This account follows that in "Carter Up Close: 'The Southern Mystique,' " *Newsweek*, 19 July 1976.

3. Jimmy Carter, *Why Not the Best?*, Bantam ed. of Broad-

man Press book (New York: Bantam Books, Inc., 1976), pp. 85-86.

4. Tom Collins, *The Search for Jimmy Carter* (Waco, Texas: Word Inc., 1976), p. 365.

5. Ibid., p. 37.

6. Ibid., pp. 36-37, and Rainone, King, and Bourne.

7. Collins, pp. 20-25.

8. Margaret Mitchell, *Gone With the Wind* (New York: Macmillan Co.: Avon Books, a division of Hearst Corp., N.Y., 1936), pp. 38-39.

9. Howard Norton and Bob Slosser, *The Miracle of Jimmy Carter* (Plainfield, N.J.: Logos International, 1976), p. 19.

10. Carter, p. 22.

11. Ibid., p. 80.

12. Schemmel, "My Son Jimmy," *Ladies Home Journal*, August 1976, p. 73.

13. Robert Scheer, "Jimmy We Hardly Know Y'All," *Playboy*, November, 1976, p. 86; transcript from television interviews on "Bill Moyers' Journal," PBS broadcast, 6 May 1976 (WETA, Washington, D.C.; WNET, New York), p. 9, quoted in *Jimmy Who?* by Leslie Wheeler (Woodbury, N.Y.: Barron's Educational Series, Inc. (1976), p. 3; and Norton and Slosser, p. 17.

14. Bill Schemmel, "My Son Jimmy," *Ladies Home Journal*, August 1976, p. 73.

15. "Carter Up Close: 'He Has a Schedule,'" *Newsweek*, 19 July 1976, p. 26.

16. Rainone, King, and Bourne, p. 88.

17. Ibid.

18. "Newsmakers," *Newsweek*, 27 December 1976, p. 37.

19. "Carter Up Close: 'The Smartest Man,'" *Newsweek*, 19 July 1976, p. 24.

20. "Carter Up Close: 'The Southern Mystique,'" p. 30.

21. Rainone, King, and Bourne, p. 86.

22. Orde Coombs, "The Hand That Rocked Carter's Cradle," *New York*, 14 June 1976, p. 41.

23. Carter, pp. 73-74.

24. Claire Safran, "The Women in Jimmy Carter's Life," *Redbook*, October 1976, p. 84.

25. Carter, p. 33.

26. Schemmel, p. 26.

27. Rainone, King, and Bourne, p. 86.

28. Ibid., pp. 51-52.

29. Schemmel, p. 145.

30. William Borders, "An Indian Town Recalls Lillian Carter Fondly. . ." *New York Times*, 21 September 1976, p. 39.

31. Scheer, p. 190. Condensation of longer monolog.

32. Rainone, King, and Bourne, p. 52; Borders, p. 39.

33. Kenneth A. Briggs, ". . . And She Has Fond Memories of Work in Its Health Clinic," *New York Times*, 21 September 1976, p. 39; Rainone, King and Bourne, p. 54; Borders, p. 39.

34. Schemmel, p. 145.

35. Rainone, King, and Bourne, p. 54.

36. Briggs, p. 39; Schemmel, p. 146.

37. Robert W. Turner, *"I'll Never Lie to You": Jimmy Carter in His Own Words* (New York: Random House, Inc.: Ballantine Books, 1975), p. 21.

38. Borders, p. 48.

39. Borders, p. 48; Schemmel, p. 146.

40. Schemmel, p. 73.

41. Ibid., p. 146.

42. Gail Sheehy, "Ladies and Gentlemen, The Second President—Sister Rosalynn," *New York*, 22 November 1976, p. 55.

43. Claire Safran, p. 84.

44. Ibid.

III. *Plains Way of Life*

1. Robert W. Turner, *"I'll Never Lie to You": Jimmy Carter in His Own Words* (New York: Random House, Inc.: Ballantine Books, 1975), pp. 100-101.

2. Jimmy Carter, *Why Not the Best?*, Bantam ed. (New York: Bantam Books, Inc., 1976), pp. 14-15.

3. Ibid., p. 67.

4. Howard Norton and Bob Slosser, *The Miracle of Jimmy Carter* (Plainfield, N.J.: Logos International, 1976), p. 25.

5. Turner, p. 15.
6. Ibid., p. 86.
7. Ibid., pp. 30-31.
8. Ibid., p. 81.
9. Carter, p. 9.
10. Ibid., p. 36.
11. Ibid., p. 28.

IV. The Unique Plains

1. Margaret Mitchell, *Gone With the Wind* (New York: Macmillan Co.: Avon Books, a Division of Hearst Corp., N.Y., 1936), p. 5.
2. Ibid., pp. 59-60.
3. This is the line from the movie of *Gone With the Wind;* in the book, the line is "My dear, I don't give a damn." [p. 1023].
4. Margaret Mitchell, *Gone With the Wind* (New York: Macmillan Co.: Avon Books, a division of Hearst Corp., N.Y., 1936), p. 95.
5. Jimmy Carter, *Why Not the Best?*, Bantam ed. of Broadman Press book (New York: Bantam Books, Inc., 1967) pp. 13-14.
6. Ibid., p. 7.

V. Vocabulary

1. The discussion of the *Atlanta Constitution* and the list of words excerpted therefrom appeared, of course, in the *New York Times*, 16 December 1976, in an article entitled "Southerners Talk Back to Yanks About Accents," by Wayne King.
2. Jimmy Carter, *Why Not the Best?*, Bantam ed. (New York: Bantam Books, Inc., 1976), p. 22.
3. Gail Sheehy, "Ladies and Gentlemen, The Second President—Sister Rosalynn," *New York*, 22 October 1976, p. 55.
4. Ibid., p. 54.

VI. *The Not-So-Plains Million-Dollar Supper*

1. Norman Mailer, "The Search for Carter," *New York Times Magazine*, 26 September 1976, p. 104.

IX. *Carter Country Tour*

1. James T. Wooten, "Plains, Ga., Presents 2 Contrasting Faces Typical of the South," *New York Times*, 20 December 1976, p. B1.

About the Authors

Beth Tartan, for 30 years a food columnist for the Winston-Salem (N.C.) *Journal & Sentinel,* is a well-known home economist throughout the South. Formerly the head of the home economics department of Salem (N.C.) College, from which she graduated, Ms. Tartan has also served as a product consultant for R. J. Reynolds Industries and as a columnist for Long Island's *Newsday.* She is also the author of two cookbooks.

Rudy Hayes is a veteran newsman, a native of Waycross, Georgia, who has been a close personal friend of Jimmy Carter and his family since the early 1960s. A graduate of the University of Georgia School of Journalism, Mr. Hayes worked for the Jacksonville (Fla.) *Journal,* and is now managing editor of the *Americus* (Ga.) *Times-Record.*

More Big Bestsellers from SIGNET

☐ **COME LIVE MY LIFE** by Robert H. Rimmer.
(#J7421—$1.95)

☐ **THE FRENCHMAN** by Velda Johnston.
(#W7519—$1.50)

☐ **THE HOUSE ON THE LEFT BANK** by Velda Johnston.
(#W7279—$1.50)

☐ **A ROOM WITH DARK MIRRORS** by Velda Johnston.
(#W7143—$1.50)

☐ **KINFLICKS** by Lisa Alther.　(#E7390—$2.25)

☐ **RIVER RISING** by Jessica North.　(#E7391—$1.75)

☐ **THE HIGH VALLEY** by Jessica North. (#W5929—$1.50)

☐ **LOVER: CONFESSIONS OF A ONE NIGHT STAND** by
Lawrence Edwards.　(#J7392—$1.95)

☐ **THE SURVIVOR** by James Herbert.　(#E7393—$1.75)

☐ **THE KILLING GIFT** by Bari Wood.　(#J7350—$1.95)

☐ **WHITE FIRES BURNING** by Catherine Dillon.
(#E7351—$1.75)

☐ **CONSTANTINE CAY** by Catherine Dillon.
(#W6892—$1.50)

☐ **FOREVER AMBER** by Kathleen Winsor.
(#J7360—$1.95)

☐ **SMOULDERING FIRES** by Anya Seton.
(#J7276—$1.95)

☐ **HARVEST OF DESIRE** by Rochelle Larkin.
(#J7277—$1.95)

THE NEW AMERICAN LIBRARY, INC.,
P.O. Box 999, Bergenfield, New Jersey 07621

Please send me the SIGNET BOOKS I have checked above. I am
enclosing $_____(check or money order—no currency
or C.O.D.'s). Please include the list price plus 35¢ a copy to cover
handling and mailing costs. (Prices and numbers are subject to
change without notice.)

Name_____

Address_____

City_____State_____Zip Code_____
Allow at least 4 weeks for delivery